D1927873

Adam and Evil

AND THE GOD WHO HATES SEX, WOMEN AND HUMAN BODIES

The Heyeokah Guru

A Dandelion Books Publication
www.dandelionbooks.net
Tempe, Arizona

Adam and Evil

The Heyeokah Guru

Copyright © 2006 by The Heyeokah Guru
ISBN-10: 1-893302-94-6
ISBN-13: 978-1-893302-94-5

All rights exclusively reserved. No part of this book may be reproduced or translated into any language or utilized in any form or by any means, electronic or mechanical, including photocopying, recording or by any information storage and retrieval system, without permission in writing from the publisher.

A Dandelion Books Publication
Dandelion Books, LLC
Tempe, Arizona

Library of Congress Cataloging-in-Publication Data
Heyeokah Guru
Adam & Evil: and the god who hates sex, women and human bodies
Library of Congress Catalog Number 2006937661
ISBN 1-893302-94-6, 978-1-893302-94-5

Cover art by Mark JF
Cover and book design by TJ Publish, www.tjpublish.com.

Disclaimer and Reader Agreement

Under no circumstances will the publisher, Dandelion Books, LLC, or author be liable to any person or business entity for any direct, indirect, special, incidental, consequential, or other damages based on any use of this book or any other source to which it refers, including, without limitation, any lost profits, business interruption, or loss of programs or information.

Though due diligence has been used in researching and authenticating the information contained in this book, Dandelion Books, LLC and the author make no representations as to accuracy, completeness, currentness, suitability, or validity of any opinions expressed in this book. Neither Dandelion Books, LLC nor the author shall be liable for any accuracy, errors, adequacy or timeliness in the content, or for any actions taken in reliance thereon.

Reader Agreement for Accessing This Book

By reading this book, you, the reader, consent to bear sole responsibility for your own decisions to use or read any of this book's material. Dandelion Books, LLC and the author shall not be liable for any damages or costs of any type arising out of any action taken by you or others based upon reliance on any materials in this book.

Printed in the United States of America

Table of Contents

Preface

I grew up in a nice, normal British middle-class family who did their best to be normal and nice and do all the 'right things.' This meant there was a lot of pressure on me to grow up into the 'right sort of' boy / man and I was sent away early to boarding school so that would happen – and because my parents understood it was the 'right thing to do.' The fact that this was blatant abandonment – at the tender age of eight no less – was quite outside their frame of reference.

Although I was not given too much religion at home, it was always there as an undertone. Humans had been thrown out of the 'Garden Of Eden' for disobedience by an angry chap called God. This meant obedience was very important in life, especially among children who must obey their 'elders and betters.' At school I was given the full religious indoctrination, with prayers every morning and evening, hymns, psalms, sermons and religious teaching, all of which suggested that a human being was not good enough for God, was born in sin and had to be urgently baptized, confirmed as a Protestant (and definitely not a Catholic!) at the age of 14 or 15, must be a good Christian, believe the Bible as the living word of God and do as he's told. And worse, to not have any sexual thoughts whatsoever, let alone any action. All of this helped me to have not just low self-esteem but virtually none at all. I was not at all violent, not good at games, and not a bully, so I had none of the usual ways of assuaging the pain of feeling inadequate or of 'proving myself.' It seemed I must be worthless and inadequate not just in the eyes of my teachers and fellows, but also God, too.

Then came puberty and 'public' school. Now to put it as politely as possible, puberty is a challenge. The body grows extra parts, with urges and agendas of their own. Religion teaches

Adam and Evil

AND THE GOD WHO HATES SEX, WOMEN AND HUMAN BODIES

that the one thing you should not do is obey any of those urges – at least not until you are safely married anyway, and even then only for procreation. Anything else is sinful, bad or even terrible, and will gain quite appalling retribution from this 'god-chap.'

But the body has a seriously powerful way of determining that its urges will, in some way or other, be heard, felt and obeyed. You have probably noticed. A furious sex drive is a natural part of being an adolescent – and a young person. But for a Christian, it is a sin to act on it or even think about it!

Public school – a strange British euphemism for an expensive private boarding school with heavy-duty righteous, religious overtones coupled with fiendish punishments where children of the privileged can be taken off their parents' hands for two thirds of the year and taught to brutalize each other – attempted to keep pupils so busy and harassed that puberty would pass by unnoticed. A dismal failure, of course. One was left simply trying to survive and get through to senior years when it becomes your job to make the new juniors have as rotten a time as you did. (Another task at which I failed, glad to say.) To put all the boys together, with no girls and little of the feminine gender at all, at the time when they are going through enormous growth into sexual beings, is quite the strangest of ideas. I mean, what on earth did the creators of such a boneheaded system expect to happen? The sexual instinct won the day – and still wins the day – as described in many biographies of those who suffered this mad 'injure-cation.'

According to religion, the ideal man – 'God's Only Son' – never married and therefore never had sex of any kind because it would have been a sin and He simply didn't sin. Hence He never had sex with a woman (a sin), never had sex with a man (even bigger sin), never had sex with Himself (big, big sin), never had an orgasm (sin outside marriage), never had an erection (sin), and could never even have had a sexual thought because that might have led to any of the above and it is a sin in and of itself.

Extraordinary!

What a load of old twaddle is that! But it means that any good Christian boy, however good he tries to be, becomes a monstrous sinner in the eyes and ears of the 'god-chap' as soon as puberty arises. I mean how many adolescent boys don't masturbate like crazy for at least some of those years – only the very low drive ones, and even then ....

What a great set-up to make all normal boys feel appallingly guilty and not good enough for this ghastly tyrant god-chap. And therefore to live in denial of their true nature and to fight inwardly against themselves. That is what happened to me. I became a raging war against my own nature as I struggled to become someone else, someone who was acceptable to God and my teachers and 'elders and betters.' Someone who fitted in with society and with what was considered 'right and proper.' I failed. Dismally.

At the age of nineteen when I felt like a totally lost soul, guilty just for being alive, isolated in the extreme, I somehow ended up at a Billy Graham meeting, at the end of which, my legs carried me to the front to 'accept Christ into my life.' I next found myself being taught by a rather extreme Christian group, who abstained from all sorts of things, such as wearing make-up (the women) and reading anything but the Bible. I was sort of impressed for a bit until I found out, under all the piety, they were just as mean-minded and bitchy as everyone else. That wonder cure lasted three weeks and I was glad to get back to a more ordinary, less pinched, level of madness.

Fortunately, I never really did believe all that crap. I felt I lived amongst mad people in a mad world and that there must be – somewhere over a very distant rainbow indeed – another way. I gave up on religion and focused on engineering. I felt that machines don't lie, they don't try to make you believe impossible things, they don't set you against yourself, they are not devious, they are true and honest – and they either work or they don't. And one can get skilled at making them work, for which I had a natural instinct.

In my thirties, I studied once a week with a yoga teacher and, for the first time, heard a philosophy that made sense, but it took a massive and wonderful mid-life crisis at age 40 to get me to stop my whole life and start over again. I found I had been right all along – I really had lived in a mad world with mad people but now I was no longer alone and isolated. There were others who felt similarly, and I received much sensible guidance and teachings that opened up for me the ways of the ancients, our ancestors who lived before the time of male-domination and all-male 'gods.'

Now, we are seeing the fruits of this collective madness all around us – the scandals of the 'celibate' priests, serious pollution of the earth and her atmosphere, over-consumption of her resources, melting of the ice-caps, junk food, the war on drugs, breakdown of families and a society that is terminal – and simply cannot go on living the way it is.

When you were a kid were you taught all about Santa Claus – the lovely, rotund old chap with a white beard and a red robe – who comes down the chimney every Christmas and leaves lovely presents for you? And then, when you were old enough, did you one day find out he didn't really exist and it was just your mom and dad?

And then were you taught about another much older, white-bearded chap called God and told *he* really, REALLY exists and that you must believe in him for the whole of the rest of your life? Were you told that he created the whole world and lives in a super place called Heaven and that if you don't believe it, you will be banished from there when you die and go to a horrible place called Hell where all the other bad people go? And have you believed what they told you, done what they told you and obeyed all the rules they told you to?

Of course, you do believe He wrote a big book called the Bible which is all His own words, don't you? And that He sent His Only Son to personally sort out the awful mess we humans made two thousand years ago and to save us from all our nasty sins? You do believe this, don't you, because if you don't, you are a nasty person and you won't get any more presents and will be sent to that nasty hell place to rot when you die!

Of course you do. After all, you're a nice and good person, aren't you, and if all the grownups tell you it is so, then it must be so, mustn't it? Big Daddy God sent His Only Begotten, Wonderful, Magical, Cuddly Son Jesus all the way down here to save the world from the terrible sins of those awful humans – our long, long ago ignorant ancestors.

And didn't he do a good job, dying so horribly just for us, just to save us from all those awful things we used to do? And aren't we so lucky and isn't the world so wonderful and nice now? And aren't we all kind to each other and hasn't it made such an enormous difference? And heaven knows how awful life would be if He hadn't come and died and saved us all. And you do believe it, don't you?

And isn't that an awful load of old cobblers?

Yet an enormous number of people still believe this 'Santa Claus-for-Grownups' chap really exists, really did write that big old book, really did have an only son who really did come and live in a body, do impossible things and really did die horribly on a cross. They seem to maintain a state of mental oblivion to human history since that time, which is a horrendous uninterrupted series of wars, inquisitions, murder, torture, deceit, lies, double-dealings, genocide, 'ethnic cleansing' (what a ghastly, lying, deceitful phrase that is) and so on, much as it had been before, only worse. We have just had a century with two massive world wars, so what on earth do the apologists think Jesus actually accomplished? Based on the actual evidence, he was a grim, lousy failure and his Big Daddy should be jolly disappointed with him. And if Big Daddy's biblical threats are anything to go by, and if the outpourings of his representatives on earth are to be taken seriously, then his Only Son will be living in the nasty hell place, forever repenting for his dismal failure. But, of course, it's all a monstrous fiction and it's time to sort out the facts, to separate the real baby from the ocean of incredibly murky, fetid, stinking bathwater.

The Jesus Story makes no sense – as I think you will find well demonstrated in this book – unless you take it as an allegory, a mythological story about our experience of life in the human form. This book is my small contribution to putting the skids under this male domination madness. We live by the stories that the collective takes to be true, and the stories are polluted, misinterpreted, skewed and screwed, and we all suffer through this. A society needs fundamental myths that support life, respect people's true nature, and remind us we are all connected to each other and to the Source, that the Real God is Everywhere, that we are all part of God, are good enough in our essence, and here to learn and grow. I hope this re-evaluation of mythological stories will help dis-empower the back-to-front teaching that has supported this collective madness.

So, now, let us start at the beginning.

The Heyeokah Guru,* England, 2006

* The Heyeokah Guru is a truthseeker, writer and workshop facilitator, living in the UK. His life has taken many twists and turns and has shown him graphically that most everything he was taught to believe in during his early formative years was crap! He constantly attempts to pull the wraps off that which is hidden and delights in pulling the rug from under those who seek to conceal, control, limit and dominate.

Chapter 1

Cultural Mythologies

A culture lives by the stories the collective tells itself, in other words, by its mythologies. The stories we tell ourselves – of how things are, why it is, how it was all created and who/what is ultimately responsible for creation – are the building blocks of what we see as 'reality,' our consensual agreement about Life, the Universe and Everything.

In the thousands of years of human evolution, there have been many such frameworks, such consensual 'realities,' ways of seeing this amazing world in which we live. Even today, we can travel to other cultures whose consensual reality is significantly different from our own. If we stay long enough and imbibe their way of seeing and being, we can have the dubious pleasure of returning to our own culture and receiving culture shock and an awakening that the givens, beliefs and assumptions of our own home land are nothing more than just that – unconscious (and semi-conscious) agreements about how to see things.

Our present Western 'civilized' culture has numerous extraordinary facets. We are creating unprecedented pollution of natural systems to a point where we may well take them beyond any recoverable balance; we are poisoning our own food so now 'organically grown' food – food grown without poisons or at least with less of them – is a significant item for many people. We have produced weapons of such mass destruction, which if used, will produce untold and quite possibly irreparable devastation to ourselves and to our home, the Earth.

Our leaders and visionaries, such as they are, have no answers. At least I haven't heard any. The Native American culture had an inbuilt teaching that one's actions should take account of seven future generations. Our culture can barely look beyond the next four years or whenever the next election is going to take place.

How long before there are so many cars that the cities and the roads just come to a stop and the air is unbreathable? How long before the skies are so full of planes that there is a pollution crisis in the upper atmosphere? One thing is sure. We live in a culture that is terminal in its present form. And at some inner level most of us know this. Our youth especially see and feel little future with things the way they are. Our mythologies are not serving us and it is time to look closely at them.

Creation Stories

If we go back far enough in human history, we come to *shamanism* (*shaman* or *saman* is a Tungus word from Siberia and means healer/visionary/person of knowledge), *paganism* (*pagan* = country dweller), and ancient earth-based cultures that embraced Mother Earth and the experience of living in a body in human form. In all the cultures I have researched, even though their creation stories seemed to differ on the surface, I found a similar fundamental understanding of how things are. The Creation IS the Creator in Manifestation. Not God did this, or God did that, or God saw it was good, or God cursed and spread his wrath, or God spoke to this or that person, etc. None of that nonsense. God, Infinite Creator, Primal Being, the One, Alone, the All-That-Is, became and is The Creation. They understood there is no separation. Infinite Creator *became* the creation and *is* the creation.

That means *all* humans are sons and daughters of God, all animals are animals of God. Trees are trees of God, planets are Planets of God and suns are Suns of God.

This is a different mythology from the religious one prevalent in the current era, so where did that one come from? There are really only three organized religions in the full sense of that. These are Judaism, Christianity and Islam. And guess what? They all have the same root and are really developments of each other rather than anything different. They all come from the Middle East and spread out across the world from there. If we define religion as 'belief in God,' Buddhism is not strictly a religion because it is a path rather than a belief system. Hinduism is a grey area because it can be called a religion yet is not a focused on specific beliefs in the way of the other three.

In the three main religions, belief in One God is central. Both Christianity and Islam teach that they have the truth and are proselytizing religions in that they feel it's their duty to convert others with the ideal that everyone will ultimately agree and believe what they say. What will then be achieved, I wonder? What else but that wonderful thing so sought by dictators and kings and leaders and psychopaths throughout the centuries:

WORLD DOMINATION THROUGH UNIFORMITY!

My Personal Mythology: The way I was told it should be

I want to look back and describe the world as I was told it was in my childhood. It went something like this:

God is a wonderful father who created the world. He lives in Heaven, which is a wonderful and perfect place somewhere up above, where nothing ever goes wrong and there is absolutely no sin or unhappiness, with his only son Jesus but with no wife and no daughters.

God is love. But he is also very judgmental and watching to see any of us who commit sins and tally them up against us, so you have to fear God even though he is love.

Good people believe in God and his only son, Jesus, who he sent to save the world.

You have to be christened as soon as you are born because if you are not and you die, your soul will go to purgatory, which is a very nasty place.

Only Christians get to Heaven because they believe in the only right God. Everyone else is mistaken, misguided and needs to be converted to Christianity for the sake of their souls.

Jesus died for our sins so, even if we commit them, so long as we believe in Jesus, we are going to be all right. We must believe Jesus died for us personally. And only if we believe in him fervently will God absolve us of our sins. When we are about to die, we must get ablution (okay, Freudian slip. In those days, that's how it sounded to me) of our sins, so even if we've committed lots of sins, we'll still be all right.

God is a nice, old, white man with a long white beard, and Jesus is a nice, young, white man with deep blue eyes, a dark beard and a comforting smile.

Women are less than men in the eyes of God and religion is more a man's thing. Monks are mainly men, saints are mainly men but some women do manage to be godly, especially nuns and unmarried women who never have sex.

Hell is a bad place down below and if you don't want to go there, you must keep trying to be godly by looking up towards heaven. And you must try not to think about, let alone touch, that place down there between your legs because it will take you straight to hell.

Sex is bad and good people do it as seldom as possible. All proper, godly people do not indulge in sex or sensuality because it is ungodly.

Jesus was born of a virginal mother which is the ideal way to be born. All Christian women are virgins on their wedding day, and all Christian married couples only commit sex when they want to have children, because to do it for any other purpose is a sin.

Enjoying sex for its own sake is a sin.

Thinking about sex is a sin.

Making yourself look sexy is a temptation to sin.

Masturbation is a big sin.

Homosexuality is a very big sin.

Fantasizing about having sex is a nasty, evil sin.

Jesus never did any of it whatsoever and nor should you (or me) and if you do, you are unfit in the eyes of God and will be punished until you stop and probably a lot longer. And if you masturbate, you'll go blind.

Quite a straight-jacket for a growing teenager, struggling to understand enormous, powerful and puzzling bodily changes. As I wrote in the Preface, the result for me was a raging internal battle between my natural nature and these dreadful ideas I was taught.

Now to Bible Creation Stories:
"In the beginning was the word and the word was with God and the word was God." (John 1:1)

Translation: In the beginning was consciousness, and consciousness was with God and consciousness was God.

Or we can substitute *awareness* or perhaps *beingness* or even *existence*. Let's try existence and see how that feels:

"In the beginning was Existence and Existence was with God, and Existence was God."

Now that puts a different flavor on it: In the beginning was existence / awareness / consciousness – and that was (and is) God.

That makes sense with the much older cultural understandings: that God is All-That-Is and Ever-Was and Ever-Will-Be. There is nothing else, never has been and never can be.

In the first Genesis story, God creates the world in seven days in a delightful apocryphal story that some religious nuts want to take as word-for-word literal truth. The human ability for absurdity amazes!

In 1650, a certain James Ussher, Archbishop of Armagh in Ireland, published the *Annales Veteris Testamenti,* which was a Church-approved 'Universal History.' It stated that God completed his creation on 21st of September, 4004 BC in the evening. To achieve such accuracy as to be able to pinpoint it to very time of day so long ago is truly astonishing! But wait: God completed his creation on a Saturday and had a rest on Sunday so does that mean he finished on Saturday 21st and rested on the first full day of existence, the 22nd, which would make it a Sunday? Or does it mean he completed everything including his rest day on 21st, making that the Sunday? We are left with a question. Was the first ever day of the Universe the 15th September so he completed the lot by 21st or was it the 16th, making his completion on the 22nd and his day of rest on the 23rd? I can just see two camps of fighting fundamentalist religionist crazies, one side firmly adhering rigidly to each of these absurd ideas!

One thing is for certain. God cannot have been British (surely not?) or he would have finished by 4 o'clock in time for a nice cup of Darjeeling tea, a cucumber sandwich (minus crusts, of course) and a piece of cinnamon cake....

However, whatever the truth might or might not be was deemed quite irrelevant in 1654 (that's only 352 years ago!) because the Vatican Council decreed that anyone found not believing that the world was created in 4004 BC was a heretic and would be treated as such. Which could mean being burned at the stake or murdered in some equally horrible church-approved way. Or, at the very least, made stateless. Comically, this edict was not repealed until 1952!

Professor Dan Smail is a medievalist with Harvard University's History Department who says that our chronology of the human race is embarrassingly out of date. He says we need to move the starting date back about 100,000 years! (*American Historical Review*, 2006.)

Quoted in *Nexus Magazine* April 2006: "According to the history books, civilization as we know it had its first stirrings in the Fertile Crescent around 4000 – 6000 BC. But as Smail points out in an article in the latest issue of the *American Historical Review*, when you consider recent (and no-so-recent) discoveries in archeology, anthropology and biology – the finding that all humankind can be traced to Africa, for example, or that humans were on the march out of that continent by roughly 100,000 BC not to mention good guesses for when language, hunting and farming arose – the fixation on a starting date of 4000 – 6000 BC begins to seem awfully arbitrary."

There is a kind of mad logic about Bishop Ussher's date, however. It must have been around that time that man – and I do mean MAN – invented 'god' in his (worst) image, drove out the more matriarchal cultures and took over the world by conquest. Since then, we have had pretty much constant war, empires building up and being destroyed, strife, competition for land and resources, killing, murder, ethnic 'cleansing' and all such evils we are familiar with. Riane Eisler wrote in detail about this in her most informative work: *The Chalice and the Blade*. The big issue right now is that if we don't grow up out of these appalling patriarchal nonsensical beliefs, we may not be around much longer.

Now in the first Bible story, God creates things in the right order and humans come last, created in God's image *male and female created he them.* (Gen 1:27)

Then comes a very much misunderstood verse, probably heavily mistranslated, but whether or not, it has been a source of ghastly human action against our planet and her kingdoms for centuries. Gen 1:28: "Be fruitful and become many and fill the earth, and *subdue it and have in subjection the fish of the sea and the flying creatures of the heavens and every living creature that is moving upon the earth.*"

So the Bible-God appears to support such monstrosities as chickens in batteries, cattle fed strange growth hormones for profit, farming practices that use animals as objects rather than beings, chemicals galore spread on the land to get more crops out, irrespective of the damage to the ecosystem. Surely there has been a serious mistranslation. To say nothing of a monstrous misuse of the Earth and her kingdoms encouraged by this statement.

Now this next bit is really strange when you think about it. In Genesis 2:7, God seems to start creation all over again and this time forms a man out of dust and woman out of his rib. Something has gone massively wrong here. We have two different creation stories and they don't agree at all. We have one story of logical creation which is followed by the Garden of Eden story where creation is put in a cockeyed order. This story has been a source of absurd back-to-front mythology and massive denigration of woman, of planet Earth, and of all things feminine.

Robert Graves, in his book *Hebrew Myths: The Book of Genesis* sums up the order of the two stories:

Genesis 1	Genesis 2
Heaven	Earth
Earth	Heaven
Light	Mist
Firmament	Man
Dry land	Trees
Grasses and trees	Rivers
Luminaries	Beasts and cattle
Sea-beasts	Birds
Birds	Woman
Cattle, creeping things, beasts	
Man and woman	

And just look where woman is placed in Genesis 2! How conveniently misogynist. And man created before the trees and rivers, beasts and cattle! What on earth was he supposed to have lived on? What a load of impossible nonsense. So let us now look in some detail at this strange second myth:

The Myth of Adam and Eve

Here are passages from the KJV of Genesis:

2:8-9: And the LORD God planted a garden eastward in Eden; and there he put the man whom he had formed. And out of the ground made the LORD God to grow every tree that is pleasant to the sight, and good for food; the tree of life also in the midst of the garden, and the tree of knowledge of good and evil.

2:15-25: And the LORD God took the man, and put him into the garden of Eden to dress it and to keep it. And the LORD God commanded the man, saying, Of every tree of the garden thou mayest freely eat:

But of the tree of the knowledge of good and evil, thou shalt not eat of it: for in the day that thou eatest thereof thou shalt surely die.

And the LORD God said, It is not good that the man should be alone; I will make him an help meet for him.

And out of the ground the LORD God formed every beast of the field, and every fowl of the air; and brought them unto Adam to see what he would call them: and whatsoever Adam called every living creature, that *was* the name thereof.

And Adam gave names to all cattle, and to the fowl of the air, and to every beast of the field; but for Adam there was not found an help meet for him.

And the LORD God caused a deep sleep to fall upon Adam, and he slept: and he took one of his ribs, and closed up the flesh instead thereof;

And the rib, which the LORD God had taken from man, made he a woman, and brought her unto the man.

And Adam said, This is now bone of my bones, and flesh of my flesh: she shall be called Woman, because she was taken out of Man.

Therefore shall a man leave his father and his mother, and shall cleave unto his wife: and they shall be one flesh.

And they were both naked, the man and his wife, and were not ashamed.

Chapter Three continues:

Now the serpent was more subtle than any beast of the field which the LORD God had made. And he said unto the woman, Yea, hath God said, Ye shall not eat of every tree of the garden?

And the woman said unto the serpent, We may eat of the fruit of the trees of the garden:

But of the fruit of the tree which is in the midst of the garden, God hath said, Ye shall not eat of it, neither shall ye touch it, lest ye die.

And the serpent said unto the woman, Ye shall not surely die:

For God doth know that in the day ye eat thereof, then your eyes shall be opened, and ye shall be as gods, knowing good and evil.

And when the woman saw that the tree was good for food, and that it was pleasant to the eyes, and a tree to be desired to make one wise, she took of the fruit thereof, and did eat, and gave also unto her husband with her; and he did eat.

And the eyes of them both were opened, and they knew that they were naked; and they sewed fig leaves together, and made themselves aprons.

And they heard the voice of the LORD God walking in the garden in the cool of the day: and Adam and his wife hid themselves from the presence of the LORD God amongst the trees of the garden.

And the LORD God called unto Adam, and said unto him, Where *art* thou?

And he said, I heard thy voice in the garden, and I was afraid, because I was naked; and I hid myself.

And he said, Who told thee that thou wast naked? Hast thou eaten of the tree, whereof I commanded thee that thou shouldest not eat?

And the man said, The woman whom thou gavest to be with me, she gave me of the tree, and I did eat.

And the LORD God said unto the woman, What is this that thou hast done? And the woman said, The serpent beguiled me, and I did eat.

And the LORD God said unto the serpent, Because thou hast done this, thou art cursed above all cattle, and above every beast of the field; upon thy belly shalt thou go, and dust shalt thou eat all the days of thy life:

And I will put enmity between thee and the woman, and between thy seed and her seed; it shall bruise thy head, and thou shalt bruise his heel.

Unto the woman he said, I will greatly multiply thy sorrow and thy conception; in sorrow thou shalt bring forth children; and thy desire shall be to thy husband, and he shall rule over thee.

And unto Adam he said, Because thou hast hearkened unto the voice of thy wife, and hast eaten of the tree, of which I commanded thee, saying, Thou shalt not eat of it: cursed is the ground for thy sake; in sorrow shalt thou eat of it all the days of thy life;

Thorns also and thistles shall it bring forth to thee; and thou shalt eat the herb of the field;

In the sweat of thy face shalt thou eat bread, till thou return unto the ground; for out of it wast thou taken: for dust thou art, and unto dust shalt thou return.

And Adam called his wife's name Eve; because she was the mother of all living.

Unto Adam also and to his wife did the LORD God make coats of skins, and clothed them.

And the LORD God said, Behold, the man is become as one of us, to know good and evil: and now, lest he put forth his hand, and take also of the tree of life, and eat, and live for ever.

Therefore the LORD God sent him forth from the garden of Eden, to till the ground from whence he was taken.

So he drove out the man; and he placed at the east of the garden of Eden Cherubims, and a flaming sword which turned every way, to keep the way of the tree of life.

~ ~ ~

There are many strange things about this myth. First the myth says Jehovah-God made the garden, put the best bit in the center, and then said to Adam, "You can't touch that."

Now come on – every parent knows what happens if you give a child a room full of toys, put the best one in the middle and say you can't play with that one! I mean whoever wrote this have must have been joking … or abysmally stupid!

Then Jehovah takes a rib from Adam and creates Eve. Well, that's the only time in any history anywhere that man has given birth to woman! On every other possible occasion, woman gives birth. Nowhere on earth, in any recorded history, has a male given birth! Never, nowhere, no when, no how! Funny story, this one. Gets stranger:

Genesis 2:25: "They were both naked and ashamed." Odd. Why should they even think of being ashamed to be just who and what they were? Where does the idea of shame come into the equation? Perhaps it comes from the writer's culture. Oh, but the Bible is the word of God isn't it, so that must mean God was ashamed! Ashamed of his own creation? Ever more peculiar!

Then along comes the cunning old Serpent, and knowingly asks Eve if God has forbidden her from eating any of the fruits of the trees. Obviously, he knows the score full well. He then suggests to Eve that God is lying and she will not die if she eats of the tree of knowledge. So she goes right ahead and eats and 'her eyes are opened.' And she doesn't die, which proves God was lying!

Now there is something rather important that would not have happened if Eve had obeyed God and *not* eaten of the Tree of the Knowledge of Good and Evil.

Think now, Ask yourself what, or who would not exist?

Something quite crucial and important would *not* exist if the Serpent hadn't successfully tempted, and Eve and Adam hadn't eaten, and their 'eyes had *not* been opened.'

I have posed this question in many talks and been amazed to get answers such as:

'There would be no evil.'

'We wouldn't have all these problems.'

'Life wouldn't be so difficult.'

'There wouldn't have been any original sin.'

All the above show a lack of understanding of life and miss the point. Totally.

Only occasionally has someone gotten the point without a lot of coaching.

What would not have happened? Think about it, but think BIG. In fact think MEGA.

Something mega important would not have happened!
Something mega important would not exist.
WHAT?
Look at the next page only when you've got it …

YOU!
AND ME!
AND THE WHOLE HUMAN RACE!

This story tells mythologically of the birth of the human race. Without the knowledge of good and evil, we are not human. Without this blessing – and challenge – of self-awareness, of knowing 'I,' we would not have the power of conscious choice and the experience of knowingly reaping the results of our actions. We would not look in a mirror and recognize our Self.

So the religionists, by screwing up this story, are actually promoting anti-evolution, actually castigating the last great evolutionary development or 'enlightenment' that took place on planet Earth, actually saying we shouldn't have become aware! Shouldn't have become human! Should have stayed animals because that's what God wanted!

And they tell us to blame the Serpent and Eve. Would they really prefer us to have stayed as animals, living in the realm of instinctual knowledge only? Are they so anti-human? So against evolution?

From the point of view of evolution, the Serpent and Eve are the *good guys* and God is the *bad guy*. Think about it ….

Animals don't know good and evil. Plants don't know good and evil. Planets, rocks and soil don't know good and evil. Only humans know good and evil. Only humans have the power of conscious choice to do good or harm. Human choice is a greatly challenging thing. We all know how much appalling harm has been done by 'good people' for the sake of 'God' with all the seeming best intentions in the world. How about the Crusades? Religious wars? Burning alive of people called heretics and witches – millions of them over centuries. ('Witch' simply meant 'wise woman and healer' before the meaning was changed to suit male power religion.) Or the total wipeout (genocide) in the twelfth century of the Cathars of Southern France by the Catholic Church? (See Chapter 6.)

Only humans bear the 'cross' of conscious choice and the responsibility that goes with it. It is the mark of being human. Funny the way our cultural myths have been messed with. How deliberately, one wonders?

Consider this phrase: 'The knowledge of good and evil.'

Many religionists understood this as meaning the knowledge of Good-God-Spirit and the knowledge of Evil-Primal-Mother-Earth.

We live in a strange world with some very strange ideas accepted as 'normal.' Look again at the everyday words GOOD and EVIL.

'Good' spells God but with a 'o' missing!
'Evil' suggests Eve - primal woman.

Have you ever really thought about this word *evil*? *Eve* is primal woman in the myth we have just told. And her name, through the misinterpretation of the Adam and Eve story, has been taken to mean all the badness in the world. Isn't that strange? How can woman be bad? Woman gives birth, all of us humans are born of woman. And yet the very name of the primal woman has been taken to represent all things bad.

The ultimate Primal woman is Mother Earth, our planet. The word 'evil' implies the doings of the Earth, our Mother. This means that all 'good' supposedly comes from 'God,' which implies the non-manifest realm, and all 'bad' comes from the Earth, the manifest realm in which we live.

Now if we look back on religious thought of the last 2,000 years and more, much of it – as I will graphically show in later chapters – has been about rejection of the earth, the body, and all things physical in favor of the heavens and all (non)things spiritual. With a mindset that does not value the physical realm, is it any wonder then that we have trashed our earth and our atmosphere, created food that contains poisons, created a mass of convenience vehicles that spew poisons out of their exhausts, and created weapons of mass destruction which, if fully used, will terminate most life on the earth. This is the essence of the culture we have inherited, have still got, and have the enormous task of changing before we take it to its ultimate deathly conclusion.

According to Gayle S. Myers (1991), it wasn't always like this:

"There is enormous archeological evidence which indicates that in older times God was thought of as a woman, the Great Mother. Revered for centuries, she was the one who gave birth to all life in the Universe. She was the fertile vessel of sexuality and creativity regarded as sacred and central to life.

"New archeological finds suggest that these early mother worshipping societies had everything necessary for civilization, from art to sanitation, farming, they manufactured and governed in cultures that were as advanced as early Greeks. The only thing missing from their societies was the weapons of warfare. Their cities, equipped with everything from temples to sewage pipes had no defensive walls and their burial sites contained no aggressive weapons. It seems they were both advanced and peaceful.

"With God as the Great Mother, the values espoused were what you would expect from a good mother. Nurturing, compassion, co-operation and an acute reverence for life were the foundation for these ancient feminine centered religions.

"Ishtar, Innana, Isis, Kali, the Great Mother was a deity of vast regions including central Europe, Mediterranean and India. Stable and thriving for 2500 years.

"Games and activities depicted in art indicate a valuing of both genders.

"Change came between 2000 and 1000 BC when destabilized by natural disasters – earthquakes and volcanic eruptions. Warlike northern nomads – Aryans – migrated south and with their weaponry easily decimated the peaceful agrarian Goddess cultures. Their religious motifs centered around the blade which they obviously regarded as sacred.

"These conquerors brought their male-dominated religion. The once ruling Great Mother was reduced to wife or consort of the ruling male deity. The values of the invaders, in contrast to nurturing, co-operation and the ability to create life, centered around power, warfare and the ability to take life."

From then on our male-dominating religious ancestors labeled the Eve-Mother-Earth-physical realms as bad, and put all good into the non-manifest, intangible realms of 'god.' And not just our ancestors; it still goes on now in this so-called 'advanced' time. No wonder we have to work so hard to find sanity in this 'developed' world when so many fell into the net and believed this abominable crap! And no wonder they banished the feminine from her rightful place in the Trinity and left only the masculine.

That means they cut their 'God' in half! The real God – Infinite Creator – is *ALL*-THAT-IS. That includes just as much feminine as masculine. A male-only God is therefore only half a God. Not only that, but Infinite Creator includes all that we label as 'good' and 'bad,' so the religionists, by making their god-chap all good (as they saw it), had to invent another chap they called 'devil' to take on the other half of their half a God!! So all they have left is a quarter of a God! Max, that is.

Through the warlike works of the believers in the all-male-god, Our Mother, the Earth, is suffering from degradation, pollution, poisoning, and numerous forms of ecological mass destruction. If she is evil, why bother about her? We live in a spiritually disconnected culture, hell bent on self-destruction.

Here's another thing – the word 'weird.' It used to mean a spiritual understanding of the flow of existence – Wyrd. The myth of Wyrd said that the 'Sisters of Wyrd' weave the web of the Universe for Eternity. The sisters – that's the females! Of course, the male domination cult couldn't have that so the meaning got changed, like so many other things.

Let us put the Serpent back in his/her place of honor, and Eve, the Great Mother, back in her place of honor, and return balance and harmony to our mythology so that the feminine and masculine can once again be in balance …

… and find a new word for *bad* instead of *eve-il.*

But there is much more wrong with this story. Jehovah-God says in Genesis 3:15-16:

'And I shall put enmity between you and the woman and between your seed and her seed. He will bruise you in the head, and you will bruise him in the heel.

To the woman he said: *"I shall greatly increase the pain of your pregnancy. In birth pangs you will bring forth children and your craving will be for your husband and he will dominate you."*

And this is 'God' speaking?

Heyeokah says: *"God save us from 'god.'"*

As the story goes on, Abraham had two sons, Cain and Abel, and later in the story they bring their offerings to Jehovah. Jehovah looks with favor on Abel who herded sheep but not on Cain who tilled the ground. Strange thing for a loving 'God' to do. Cain, in rage, then kills Abel. (Genesis 4)

Cain becomes a fugitive and goes to live east of Eden with – guess who – *other people!*

That's right – *other people!* So the Garden of Eden story is not about the only people and Jehovah-God is not the only God, but just a minor bit-player, one of many. Note that the word *Elohim*, which was used to refer to God(s), is a plural term. It is very important to realize that only certain people have been 'thrown out of the garden' and live with all that shame and guilt. There are lots of *other people* who still live on the earth as a garden and do not carry that incredible burden – shame, guilt, blame and the awful concept that they are evil – with them.

Imagine living without all that guilt! The death of Jesus doesn't hang on your shoulders! You don't have to believe in him or else you will be damned and go to hell. You are descended from other people! Freedom! That's my choice!

IT'S TIME TO WAKE UP!

Chapter 2

Original Sin

"Jesus died to 'save you from your sins.'"
"Really? Just what exactly is he supposed to save me from?"

Let's start by looking at the word 'sin.' In Aramaic, the word 'sin' meant 'missing the mark.' It was an archery term used when missing the center of a target, missing a point, missing a kill. Put another way, it meant being off center, off the mark, making a mistake.

A person who misses the mark, who is off-center, who makes a mistake, is a normal person. Who doesn't make mistakes? Putting that in the old language, one can ask: 'Who isn't a sinner?'

Answer: No one! We all make mistakes, we all get off-center, we all miss the mark. Hopefully we hit as often than miss. And the more we live and study life and learn to live well, the more we hit the mark and the fewer mistakes we make. That, in the old language, is to sin less. An airplane flying from, let's say, London to New York, spends over 90% of its time off-course, but by regular course corrections, gets there just fine. The airplane 'sins' for 90% of its journey, yet succeeds perfectly in doing its job! So it is with ourselves as we continuously learn to correct our course.

But now if one man dies for the sins of all others, what does that mean? That all your previous mistakes (sins) are eradicated? That you no longer need to learn from life? That you now have no need for further knowledge, further experience, further learning, further exploring? That He did it all for you? This makes no sense whatsoever. A life without learning, growth, development, exploration, change, flowering, and all that that implies, is no life, so one might as well pack up and die.

This nonsense makes all personal development and growth unnecessary and irrelevant. If we are not here to grow and develop, then what are we born for? Forget schools and universities, books and study, knowledge and wisdom, and just replace it all with a set of rigid dogmatic beliefs! AAH! But they already did that and created the Dark Ages by burning books and libraries and enforcing ignorance on pain of death. Message: "Read *only* the Bible, stay pig ignorant and be controlled by us."

Mind you, there is one hell of a problem for 'true believers.' What about all the billions of humans who existed before Jesus? He wasn't around then for them to believe in and he certainly wasn't around to 'save' them. Well, I guess that means either they were condemned willy-nilly or else they had to save themselves. Apparently the Roman Catholic Church had a big problem with this, and to solve it, they said that all good Christians (that means good rigid dogmatic Catholics only, folks) who lived before Jesus went into a sort of limbo holding pattern until the end of time. It seems someone twigged that Moses, Abraham and all sorts of worthies had been in Catholic 'limbo' for a massively long time, and just recently the new pope thought it was time they were let out … only it still leaves the churches teaching on this matter rather in – er – limbo.

It seems also that the Catholic Church holds that however you sin while in life, so long as you confess and repent on your deathbed and commit yourself to Jesus – as a committed Catholic, of course – you can still get to this heaven place when you shuffle off the mortal coil. What a load of old manipulation and bribery! Do as thou wilt until the last, and just be sure to change your tune on your deathbed. Easy!

Popes of old used to increase their coffers by selling 'indulgences,' so there was no need to get too serious about the daily problems of sin. (Sounds just like the recent UK scandal of selling dukedoms for political donations.)

What astonishes me is that no one seems to see what a total and utter ridiculing of the Creator this is. It makes 'God' into the most appalling, small-minded, bigoted, unseeing, unfeeling moron of a human-like being. Male, of course. And this is supposed to be the Creator of the Whole Universe. What an insult of megalithic proportions! What imbecility!

This whole original sin idea is really weird. Isn't it a seriously peculiar idea that all humans should be born in sin? Have you ever looked properly at a new born child in its natural beauty? Doesn't it move something in your heart when you see a very little child? Can you be serious and say this child is born in sin? What a ridiculous, damaging, absurd, abominable tenet this is. How *huge* has been the emotional damage done to people who believed such an appallingly soul-negating concept. How much hurt and pain has this abomination caused in the last few thousand years? Some well-known names subscribed to this absurdity:

In the 1st century, Tertullian (Quintus Florens Tertullianus, 155-220, influential Christian writer and father of the church) wrote: *"Each of you women is an Eve … You are the gate of Hell, you are the temptress of the forbidden tree; you are the first deserter of the divine law."*

He also declared: *"Chastity is a means whereby a man will traffic in a mighty substance of sanctity."*

And that the sexual act rendered even marriage 'obscene.' He must have had a lot of sexual frustration in his life!

From the 4th century, Catholic theologian St. Augustine said: *"Do not believe, or say, or teach, that the unbaptized infant can be forgiven original sin—not if you wish to be a Catholic."*

And from Psalm 51:5: *"Behold I was shapen in wickedness: in this sin hath my mother conceived me."*

St Jerome: *"Regard everything as poison which bears within it the seed of sensual pleasure."*

And in the 16th century, Martin Luther decreed: *"If a woman grows weary and at last dies from childbearing, it matters not. Let her die from bearing, she is there to do it."*

Misogyny of a rare sort. Perhaps he hated his mother! Here is another piece of horrible anti-woman preaching from a New England minister, circa 1800's (reported by Barbara G Walker in *The Woman's Encyclopedia of Myths and Secrets,* Harper and Row, 1983): *"Chloroform is a decoy of Satan, apparently offering itself to bless women; but in the end it will harden society and rob God of the deep earnest cries which arise in time of trouble, for help."*

John Calvin (1509-64) clearly hated children and women. Reading his stuff makes you wonder just what sort of mothering he must have had, to say nothing of a love-life. Here is a nice example of his so-called 'wisdom': *"Even infants bring their condemnation with them from the mother's womb … their whole nature is … a seed of sin … and odious and abominable to God."*

A baby odious and abominable to God? Just what on earth does he think of his god? This guy was seriously twisted. Furthermore, this absurd doctrine means that babies must be baptized in order for them to have a chance at salvation, or else they cannot go to 'heaven' when they die. And this means if a fetus is aborted, or miscarried, it will never, ever, have a chance to be 'saved'! Hence the anti-abortion lobby. And all because of maniacal, misguided, sexually frustrated preachers of older times. Clearly then, anti-abortionists must fanatically defend fetuses at all costs. But they don't have to be the slightest bit concerned with the already-born because it doesn't matter if people are poor or suffering or how hellish the conditions of their lives are. The only thing that matters is that they get born so they will have a chance at 'eternal salvation.'

> *"Even though anesthesia began to be used in 1846, it was not routinely administered to women in childbirth for almost 40 years, because many doctors followed the biblical teaching that women must suffer in childbirth."*
>
> — Gaylor, 1981 and 1993

Disgusting! This seems to be predicated on Genesis 3:16 where 'god' says: *'To the woman he said: "I shall greatly increase the pain of your pregnancy; in birth pangs you will bring forth children, and your craving will be for your husband, and he will dominate you."*

'God' really shows his colors ... if you believe this really is god speaking.

How about the words of a certain preacher called William Branham who died as recently as 1965: *"Woman is the filthiest being there is. Woman is the vessel of sin. Woman is lower than an animal. Woman is lower than a pig."*

Yes, that's *1965*, folks, a mere forty odd years ago. Apparently he founded his own fundamentalist Pentacostal community extension mission somewhere in Latin America. Well, pity any poor women forced – or worse still, brainwashed enough – to be in his congregation and listening to him.

Orthodox Christians not only saw woman as lesser and filthy but also the act of birth itself, so that after giving birth, a woman had to have a 40-day (for a boy child) or an 80-day (for a girl child) purifying or 'churching' in order to be re-admitted to the church and 'proper Christian society.' It seems that some thought even the Virgin Mary needed to be purified after giving birth to Jesus!

Incredible – but as I say – this is our history. Compare it with this from Thom Hartmann, *The Last Hours of Ancient Sunlight* (p303, Harmony Books, 1999): "Hundreds of thousands of years of human history – and the modern day 'primitive' people we can still find alive on the earth – tell us that the 'conventional wisdom' that 'man's innate nature is evil and dominating' is a lie, a sickness unique to our culture, and a relatively recent sickness in the long history of the human race. **Instead, we are born to an innate knowledge and awe of the divine in all creation, and our first and most basic instincts are compassion and love."** (My emphasis)

Now that is a sensible way of seeing our relationship to life and to Creation. What a pity you can't find anything like that in the Bible.

Let us look now at the sexual mores put out by Churchianity – or as I prefer to say it – *church-inanity.* If we take the Catholic version as the original, it basically says: "No birth control, no abortion, no masturbation, so sex outside marriage and preferably none at all within marriage unless you are intending pregnancy."

Not much left to enjoy! Sorry, you shouldn't enjoy it either; just do it as a duty when you have to!

St Augustine's recommendations for marriage were: *"Husbands love your wives but love them chastely. Insist on the work of the flesh only in such measure as is necessary for the procreation of children. Since you cannot beget children in any other way,* ***you must descend to it against your will****, for it is the punishment of Adam."*

Isn't that lovely? *'Descend to it against your will.'* "Darling, come and descend with me against your will, let us suffer together that God may quickly grant us a child without too much more of this unchristly copulation curfuffle!" I mean – really! Back in the Victorian era in some parts of society, it was customary to put a sheet with a small hole in it between you when you 'descended to it.' Also a Jewish habit, I understand.

What on earth is a normal, young mortal supposed to do with their natural sexual energy? Work against it? 'Confess' it every week as if it were 'bad'? It seems to me to be a perfect recipe for misery, unhappiness and serious inner conflict, leading to alcoholism, pornography, rape, violence, war, strife and evils of all sorts. Just about what we've got, in fact.

History tells that Augustine had problems with his own sexuality. Apparently he was promiscuous in his youth and had an illegitimate child who he abandoned. He came to the view that sex was intrinsically evil. Oh, what guilt can do! Here he is again, dumping his problem on everyone: *"Who can control this when its appetite is aroused? No one!"*

Well he couldn't, obviously. The fact that others can while he couldn't must have been outside his awareness, and he simply projected his own incompetence onto everybody. He goes on: *"In the very moment of the appetite, it has no mode corresponding to the will."*

Of course, it doesn't. It takes us beyond rationality and will into a wonderful, fabulous, All-One place. But Augustine, you idiot, you did have choice as to when to go with the appetite and when not. He goes further: *"This diabolical excitement of the genitals is evidence of Adam's original sin which is transmitted from the mother's womb and taints all human beings with sin."*

So just because this 'saint' couldn't control himself, he dumps sin and guilt onto all women – and all who dare to enjoy sex – and with an incredibly long-term effect, too, because we are still suffering from the aftermath of this griping nonsense today. And this guy is a 'saint'?

If you feel a smidgen upset by that comment, try this piece of dubious Augustinian wisdom: "… *man has been naturally so created that it is advantageous for him to be submissive, but disastrous for him to follow his own will, and not the will of his creator.*"

Well, there is apparent sense in that in as much as he is recommending following the guidance of the Creator, but we know what he really means is submit to the will of the Church. And when you look at the qualities of the repressive, domineering imposter-god he wants you to obey, it's nothing more than robbing the people of their rights and making them mind-controlled slaves. I have read that Augustine thought that God spent time before creating the world in preparing a place of punishment! Oh, Marquis de Sade, where were you then? You would have been in heaven with Augustine and his 'god'!

We all know this crap lives on and infects the minds of many cultures today. Here, much later, is the Bishop of Chartres, Sir John of Salisbury quoted in *The Natural Inferiority of Women: "Who except one bereft of sense would approve sensual pleasure itself, which is illicit, wallows in filthiness, is something that men censure, and that God without doubt condemns?"*

Today we live in a society that is severely out of balance with sexuality, but it's important to remember it's because of centuries of crazy religious repression, and it will not be healed by more of the same.

Here is ex-Dominican friar and Catholic priest, Matthew Fox, from *Confessions: The Making of a Postdenominational Priest* (Harper Collins, San Francisco, 1996): "This pope and his self-appointed German Mafia headed by Cardinal Ratzinger (now Pope Benedict 16th) will have to face the judgment of history (and very likely God also) for their preoccupation with sexual morality; active encouragement of population explosion by forbidding birth control; headlong pursuit of Augustine's theology of sexuality; conscious destruction and systemic dismantling of the Liberation Theology movement with the encouragement of the CIA; the effort to eliminate theology and replace it with ideology by spreading fear among theologians; the rigid sticking to celibacy as a requisite for being a priest (as well as the requisite of having exclusively male genitals) … oh, yes, and criticizing yoga – in a prolonged effort to render fascism fashionable."

The religio-fascist repression that so many people have lived under all these centuries has been released to some degree within the last fifty or more years and the results are mixed to say the least. Not surprising, as there is no proper guidance and no knowledgeable guides. In the very old days, this used to be done by the elders who had some wisdom and knowledge from long life experience, but we don't have those today … or incredibly few. Most of our elders are 'old people.' So our youth have no sensible guidance and must muddle through somehow as best they can.

Consider the time of puberty. How was puberty for you? Were you instructed by the priest in how to use your newly developing body? Told what the new and growing bits were for? How to work with this incredible energy in good, healthy, loving ways? How to give and receive pleasure beautifully? I doubt it, but if you had been a Native American living in a tribe that had maintained its balance and harmony with the Universe and with its ancestral teachings, the chances are you would have been taught at puberty by a tribal elder-teacher – male or female appropriately – who would have instructed you physically, emotionally, mentally and spiritually in how to use and develop this energy in beauty, how to access beautiful states of consciousness with it, how to create or not create children, how to give and receive joy and happiness with a loving partner. Consider what an incredible difference that could have made to your life.

IT CERTAINLY WOULD HAVE TO MINE!

Male literalist religions have demonized sex as something to control, limit, restrict, bottle-up and de-humanize. What is so ridiculous is that it's a demonization of the very energy though which we are all created! Religion demonizes the immensely powerful energy of sex and then offers to 'save' us from all the resulting problems they created in the first place! Well, it has kept them in business for thousands of years, but at what cost to the human race?

Natural sex takes us into the realms of the transcendental, of the unknown, the feminine, the chaotic because, by its very nature, it takes us beyond control of the mind into a place where spirit can enter and move us. Good sex raises our energy from the base chakra (base of the spine) right up to the lotus (top of the head) and brings us to a place of openness to the Powers of Creation. Control and limit the expression of the base energy and you limit all the other energy in a person. People with low energy and low self-esteem are insecure, more obedient and less trouble than those with high energy who feel good about themselves. By putting normal people at war with themselves, by inhibiting their natural sexual, creative vibrant self-expression, you achieve what Stalinists, Hitlerists and fascists of all shapes and sizes have sought to do throughout history … and with far less trouble and cost.

In my ignorance of youth, I picked up the fundamental Christian belief system, especially about sex. Today I feel ashamed that I could have been so duped. I grew up terrified of my own sexuality and power, and walked my adolescent world on eggshells like a real wimp. I have to admit to still holding a measure of anger and resentment against those who taught me such garbage, and the religious progenitors of the garbage itself. Perhaps that is obvious in the text of this book. Well, at least I'm now putting it to good use!

Sex and Swear Words

Isn't it weird that many of the commonly used words to describe the sexual act in the English language are also considered to be swear words? Doesn't that say volumes about the Anglo-Saxon Christian attitudes to sexuality?

The sexual act is the greatest single creative act we can do. We have 'weapons of mass creation' with which we can do no less than reproduce ourselves. Furthermore Cosmic Design (God) has seen to it that enormous pleasure accompanies this act when it is done rightly, and enormous urges propel us regularly in its direction! Yet our words commonly used for those highly pleasurable 'weapons of mass creation' and the act they involve are desultory if not downright insulting. This is extraordinary when you think about it, and shows how far down the road to mass craziness we have come.

The words for the 'weapons of mass destruction,' on the other hand, hold no such reservation. They are easily used and no one is offended by them. So if you cross my boundaries and anger me and I say to you: "Nuke off, you warhead," you will probably laugh and are certainly unlikely to take offence. Whereas if I translate that directly into the nearest appropriate words of mass creation and say: "Fuck off, you dickhead," you will probably be stung to respond and may well feel offended.

We consider destruction with equanimity yet equate sexual creation with embarrassment, ridicule, offence and negativity. How come? Heyeokah says it is all part of our upside-down religious heritage, and it is way time for re-evaluation.

Consider, for a moment, the word 'fuck.' It comes from the 18th century when people were jailed for adultery and sexual misdemeanors, and their 'crime' was recorded on police paperwork as: 'For Unlawful Carnal Knowledge.' This was abbreviated on the notice outside their cell to F.U.C.K. Then there are words like bonk, wank, (get) stuffed, and so on. The male organ is derogatorily known as prick, tool, willy, john-thomas, dick, etc, and the female organ as cunt (from cuni, Latin for birth channel, hence cuni-lingus), hole, pussy. All these words are used in a demeaning way. By contrast, the Cherokee words are Tipili (male) and Tupouli (female) and the Hindi words are Vajra and Yoni and they are always used in an affirming, respectful and honoring way.

The really bad things that happen to us are to do with war, killing, murder, ravaging, savagery, brutality, torture, destruction, decimation, so wouldn't it make more sense if our swear words reflected this? Here are some suggestions for more relevant swear words: get nuked! / bomb off! / eat anthrax! / go jump on a mine! / tank off, you tanker / get gunned! / You'll have to be genetically modified / go get tortured / nuke 'em till they glow. Add your own …

A Little History Lesson

(note: his-story, not her-story!)

- 325 AD: The Council of Nicaea decreed that no priest will be allowed to marry after ordination.
- 385 AD: Pope Siricius decreed that priests married before ordination must not make love with their wives afterwards. (Must have been some slippage in getting the Nicaean Decree out to the provinces!)
- 553 AD: Emperor Justinian convened the Second Synod council of Constantinople and forced through the doctrine: "If anyone assert the fabulous pre-existence of souls and shall submit to the monstrous doctrine that follows from it, let him be … excommunicated." That meant no more Christians could now have any past lives!
- Pope Gregory ('The Great,' 590-604 AD) decreed that all sexual desire was sinful and only for producing children.

- 1074 AD: Pope Gregory VII decreed all priests must be celibate.
- Late 20th century: The truth of what 'celibate' priests really did with their sexual energy for years starts to become public knowledge.

Note that St Peter the 'Rock,' on whom the church was said to be founded, was said to be a married man.

No wonder we're all crazy and have to work so hard to find sanity in this 'developed' world when so many fell into the net and believed all this stuff!

And no wonder they banished the feminine from her rightful place in the Trinity and left only the masculine (more in chapter 8). The feminine qualities of compassion, nurturing, caring, supporting and mutual trust went out of the window to be replaced by competitiveness, domination, lack of self-worth and the perceived need to 'prove' yourself, a sense of total lack of support, of loneliness and isolation. Just what I experienced at all-male boarding schools where a boy's only value was perceived in what he could win. Here is an aboriginal view described by Thom Hartmann in his illuminating book *The Last Hours of Ancient Sunlight* (p.242):

"When European missionaries taught Australian Aborigine hunter/gatherers how to play football (soccer) back in the early 1900s, the Aboriginal children played until both sides had equal scores: that was when the game was over, in their mind, and it boggled the British missionaries who taught them the game. The missionaries worked for over a year to convince the children that there should be winners and losers. The children lived in a matrilineal society that valued cooperation; the Englishmen came from a patriarchal society which valued domination."

~ ~ ~

With the replacement of the matriarchal cooperation and community by the patriarchal competition and domination, the human race is suffering from soul-loss on a gigantic scale. As a direct result of this, our Earth-Mother is suffering from degradation, pollution, poisoning, and so many forms of ecological mass destruction. If she is seen as evil and inferior, why should men (and I do mean *men*) bother about her?

I don't understand what on earth these people actually think of 'God.' They ascribe all sorts of hateful, judgmental and appalling behavior to 'Him' and then say he is the great creator and boss-man of the world. (Well, not my world, I tell you that for sure.) Children born in sin? A woman's body the seed bed of sin?

This crap would be an incredible insult to anyone, never mind to the Creator-Of-All-Life. Imagine a Creator who puts the most powerful desire within us to enjoy sex and the most excellent rewards of loving enjoyment for doing so and then says it is a 'sin' and you mustn't do it unless you absolutely have to.

Confused? Sadistic? I can't find printable words to describe my feelings. I expect some nincompoop to come waving a Bible at me and saying, "But this is the Word of God. This is what He says."

Well, have you ever read the Bible? I mean with a modicum of intelligence, not just like a parrot. It is about the most contradictory book you can find anywhere. And violent, judgmental, warlike! If you do a personality profile on 'God,' you find a violent, paranoid, war-obsessed, schizophrenic, domineering, misogynistic egotist of a type you (well me, anyway) wouldn't *want* to know! Is this the 'god' you really want to believe in, to worship, to honor? No wonder the world is in a parlous state.

So let's hear from this 'god-chap' himself in the next chapter on the 'verbatim word of God.'

Chapter 3

The Bible Is the Word of God?

I remember many years ago being asked / told many times: "Of course, you *do believe* the Bible is the word of God, don't you?"

More a command than a question. And once they had got a yes out of me (and I didn't know any better in those days), they then proceeded to bludgeon me with selected texts that made me into a horrendous sinner and guilty for all sorts of wrong-doing, wrong thinking and devilish beliefs and quite unfit to think for myself. So naturally I should go to their church and belittle myself in front of their altar – or whatever demeaning actions they deemed good for my soul and captivating of my energy. By the time they had finished with me, any minuscule tendencies I might have had towards self-esteem or self-confidence were well and truly swept under the carpet.

Well, let's look at the words of God and see just what this God-chap actually says.

First here is a verbatim introduction from one of those cozy Christian Bible societies:

"God reveals Himself to mankind through His Word. The Bible is a book about God and His relationship with human beings. Where do you fit in His plan? The Scriptures contain a long history of God's revelation of Himself to man—from Adam to Moses down through the apostles and the early Church. In contrast to many human assumptions, the Bible communicates a true picture of God."

So let's have it – (drum roll, please).

God in His Own Words

One might expect the Bible to be full of the words of a loving, all-mighty, compassionate God-figure. But if you read it, you find it is full of a god-chap who judges, kills, murders, supports slavery and even, at times, rape. Read on and see for yourself:

Kill people who don't listen to priests:

Anyone arrogant enough to reject the verdict of the judge or of the priest who represents the LORD your God must be put to death. Such evil must be purged from Israel. (Deut. 17:12 NLT)

Death for hitting your father or mother:

Whoever strikes his father or mother shall be put to death. (Exodus 21:15 NAB)

Death for cursing parents:

1) If one curses his father or mother, his lamp will go out at the coming of darkness. (Proverbs 20:20 NAB)

2) All who curse their father or mother must be put to death. They are guilty of a capital offense. (Leviticus 20:9 NLT)

Death for adultery:

If a man commits adultery with another man's wife, both the man and the woman must be put to death. (Leviticus 20:10 NLT)

Death for fornication:

A priest's daughter who loses her honor by committing fornication and thereby dishonors her father also, shall be burned to death. (Leviticus 21:9 NAB)

Kill nonbelievers:

They entered into a covenant to seek the Lord, the God of their fathers, with all their heart and soul; and everyone who would not seek the Lord, the God of Israel, was to be put to death, whether small or great, whether man or woman. (2Chronicles 15:12-13 NAB)

Kill homosexuals:

If a man lies with a male as with a women, both of them shall be put to death for their abominable deed; they have forfeited their lives. (Leviticus 20:13 NAB)

(Note: Matthew Fox, in his Thesis 72 states: *"Since homosexuality is found amongst 464 species and in 8% of the human population, it is altogether natural for those who are born that way and is a gift from God and nature to the greater community."* Thesis 73 states: *"Homophobia in any form is a serious sin against love of neighbor, a sin of ignorance of the richness and diversity of God's Creation as well as a sin of exclusion."*

Heyeokah says: All the male dominated religions are homophobic and use homosexuals as convenient scapegoats – a common enemy – to unite their followers in bigotry. The Native American people, a matriarchal and a more spiritually advanced society, and other similar pre-god-chap cultures, saw homosexuals as people who Creator-God had relieved of the task of parenting and therefore had a special purpose for in life.

Kill fortunetellers:

A man or a woman who acts as a medium or fortuneteller shall be put to death by stoning; they have no one but themselves to blame for their death. (Leviticus 20:27 NAB)

Kill false prophets:

If a man still prophesies, his parents, father and mother, shall say to him, "You shall not live, because you have spoken a lie in the name of the Lord." When he prophesies, his parents, father and mother, shall thrust him through. (Zechariah 13:3 NAB)

This next one is my favorite. It really sums up the arrogant, angry, egotistical, belligerent, bullying, violent, murderous, vengeful, condemning, punishing, psychopathic monster that the nice people of the Bible Society want us to worship as our Creator.

Kill the entire town if one person worships another god:

Suppose you hear in one of the towns the LORD your God is giving you that some worthless rabble among you have led their fellow citizens astray by encouraging them to worship foreign gods. In such cases, you must examine the facts carefully. If you find it is true and can prove that such a detestable act has occurred among you, you must attack that town and completely destroy all its inhabitants, as well as all the livestock. Then you must pile all the plunder in the middle of the street and burn it. ***Put the entire town to the torch as a burnt offering to the LORD your God.*** *That town must remain a ruin forever; it may never be rebuilt. Keep none of the plunder that has been set apart for destruction. Then the LORD will turn from his fierce anger and be merciful to you. He will have compassion on you and make you a great nation, just as he solemnly promised your ancestors. "The LORD your God will be merciful only if you obey him and keep all the commands I am giving you today, doing what is pleasing to him."* (Deut. 13:13-19 NLT)

Kill women who are not virgins on their wedding night:

But if this charge is true (that she wasn't a virgin on her wedding night), *and evidence of the girls virginity is not found, they shall bring the girl to the entrance of her father's house and there her townsman shall stone her to death, because she committed a crime against Israel by her unchasteness in her father's house. Thus shall you purge the evil from your midst.* (Deuteronomy 22:20-21 NAB)

And what about men who are not virgins on their wedding night? No mention, of course!

Kill followers of other religions:

Suppose a man or woman among you, in one of your towns that the LORD your God is giving you, has done evil in the sight of the LORD your God and has violated the covenant by serving other gods or ***by worshipping the sun, the moon, or any of the forces of heaven, which I have strictly forbidden****. When you hear about it, investigate the matter thoroughly. If it is true that this detestable thing has been done in Israel, then that man or woman must be taken to the gates of the town and stoned to death.* (Deuteronomy 17:2-5 NLT)

Isn't that astonishing! The god-chap is against worship of the forces of heaven, against the sun, the moon – interesting and weird. Isn't God supposed to have created the sun and the moon? I mean – without them, where are we?

Kill people for working on the Sabbath:

The LORD then gave these further instructions to Moses: 'Tell the people of Israel to keep my Sabbath day, for the Sabbath is a sign of the covenant between me and you forever. It helps you to remember that I am the LORD, who makes you holy. Yes, keep the Sabbath day, for it is holy. Anyone who desecrates it must die; anyone who works on that day will be cut off from the community. Work six days only, but the seventh day must be a day of total rest. I repeat: Because the LORD considers it a holy day, anyone who works on the Sabbath must be put to death.' (Exodus 31:12-15 NLT)

And there is no messing with the god-chap's very convenient instructions when instructing Joshua on how the Israelite army should deal with a conquered people:

'Now therefore kill every male among the little ones, and kill every woman that hath known man by lying with him. But all the women children, that have not known man by lying with him, keep alive for yourselves.' (Numbers 31: 17-18)

So God advocates killing everyone except the young, virginal women who you can keep for yourselves, fellas. This surely is quite the most 'convenient' 'god' ever invented. Ooh, sorry, I forgot, the Bible is the Word of God so it must be the right thing to do if God says so…. Well, lead me to the virgins and I will do my best to comply….

God supports the murder of children:

The glory of Israel will fly away like a bird, for your children will die at birth or perish in the womb or never even be conceived. Even if your children do survive to grow up, I will take them from you. It will be a terrible day when I turn away and leave you alone. I have watched Israel become as beautiful and pleasant as Tyre. But now Israel will bring out her children to be slaughtered." O LORD, what should I request for your people? I will ask for wombs that don't give birth and breasts that give no milk." The LORD says, "All their wickedness began at Gilgal; there I began to hate them. I will drive them from my land because of their evil actions. I will love them no more because all their leaders are rebels. The people of Israel are stricken. Their roots are dried up; they will bear no more fruit. ***And if they give birth, I will slaughter their beloved children.*** *"* (Hosea 9:11-16 NLT)

Kill men, women, and children:

Then I heard the LORD say to the other men, "Follow him through the city and kill everyone whose forehead is not marked. Show no mercy; have no pity! Kill them all – old and young, girls and women and little children. But do not touch anyone with the mark. Begin your task right here at the Temple." So they began by killing the seventy leaders. "Defile the Temple!" the LORD commanded. ***"Fill its courtyards with the bodies of those you kill! Go!"*** *So they went throughout the city and did as they were told.* (Ezekiel 9:5-7 NLT)

Kill old men and young women:

"You are my battle-ax and sword," says the LORD. ***"With you I will shatter nations and destroy many kingdoms. With you I will shatter armies, destroying the horse and rider, the chariot and charioteer. With you I will shatter men and women, old people and children, young men and maidens. With you I will shatter shepherds and flocks, farmers and oxen, captains and rulers.*** *As you watch, I will repay Babylon and the people of Babylonia for all the wrong they have done to my people in Jerusalem," says the LORD. "Look, O mighty mountain, destroyer of the earth! I am your enemy," says the LORD. "I will raise my fist against you, to roll you down from the heights. When I am finished, you will be nothing but a heap of rubble. You will be desolate forever. Even your stones will never again be used for building. You will be completely wiped out," says the LORD.* (Jeremiah 51:20-26)

(Note that after God promises the Israelites a victory against Babylon, the Israelites actually get their butts kicked by them. So much for an all-knowing and all-powerful god!)

Kill the children of sinners:

If even then you remain hostile toward me and refuse to obey, I will inflict you with seven more disasters for your sins. I will release ***wild animals that will kill your children*** *and destroy your cattle, so your numbers will dwindle and your roads will be deserted.* (Leviticus 26:21-22 NLT)

God says: Kill, war, famine, destroy, horror:

Then the LORD said to me, "Even if Moses and Samuel stood before me pleading for these people, I wouldn't help them. Away with them! Get them out of my sight! And if they say to you, 'But where can we go?' tell them, ***'This is what the LORD says: Those who are destined for death, to death; those who are destined for war, to war; those who are destined for famine, to famine; those who are destined for captivity, to captivity.'*** *"I will send four kinds of destroyers against them," says the LORD. "I will send the sword to kill, the dogs to drag away, the vultures to devour, and the wild animals to finish up what is left. Because of the wicked things Manasseh son of Hezekiah, king of Judah, did in Jerusalem, I will make my people an object of horror to all the kingdoms of the earth."* (Jeremiah 15:1-4 NLT) I'm speechless!

Kill your neighbors:

(Moses) *stood at the entrance to the camp and shouted, "All of you who are on the LORD's side, come over here and join me." And all the Levites came. He told them,* ***"This is what the LORD, the God of Israel, says: Strap on your swords! Go back and forth from one end of the camp to the other, killing even your brothers, friends, and neighbors."*** *The Levites obeyed Moses, and about three thousand people died that day. Then Moses told the Levites, "Today you have been ordained for the service of the LORD, for you obeyed him even though it meant killing your own sons and brothers. Because of this, he will now give you a great blessing."* (Exodus 32:26-29)

Rape is okay:

God seems, if we are to seriously believe the Bible, to condone and even approve of rape.

As you approach a town to attack it, first offer its people terms for peace. If they accept your terms and open the gates to you, then all the people inside will serve you in forced labor. But if they refuse to make peace and prepare to fight, you must attack the town. When the LORD your God hands it over to you, kill every man in the town. But ***you may keep for yourselves all the women, children****, livestock, and other plunder.* ***You may enjoy the spoils of your enemies that the LORD your God has given you.*** (Deut. 20:10-14)

They attacked Midian just as the LORD had commanded Moses, and they killed all the men... (On their return) Moses, Eleazar the priest, and all the leaders of the people went to meet them outside the camp. But Moses was furious with all the military commanders who had returned from the battle. "Why have you let all the women live?" he demanded. "These are the very ones who followed Balaam's advice and caused the people of Israel to rebel against the LORD at Mount Peor. They are the ones who caused the plague to strike the LORD's people. ***Now kill all the boys and all the women who have slept with a man. Only the young girls who are virgins may live; you may keep them for yourselves.*** (Numbers 31:7-18 NLT)

Death to adulterers:

If within the city a man comes upon a maiden who is betrothed, and has relations with her, you shall bring them both out of the gate of the city and there stone them to death: the girl because she did not cry out for help though she was in the city, and the man because he violated his neighbor's wife. (Deut. 22:23-24)

And this extraordinary demand:

If a man is caught in the act of raping a young woman who is not engaged, he must pay fifty pieces of silver to her father. Then he must marry the young woman because he violated her, and he will never be allowed to divorce her. (Deuteronomy 22:28-29)

I mean, just what sort of a married life are they likely to have?

Ritual human sacrifices are okay:

In Genesis, Abraham is ordered by God to sacrifice his son: "Take your son, your only son – yes, Isaac, whom you love so much – and go to the land of Moriah. Sacrifice him there as a burnt offering on one of the mountains, which I will point out to you." (Genesis 22:1-18)

Abraham takes his own son up on a mountain and builds an altar upon which to burn him. He even lies to his son and has him help build the altar. Then Abraham ties his son to the altar and puts a knife to his throat. He then hears God tell him this was just a test of his faith. However, God still wanted to smell some burnt flesh so he tells Abraham to burn a ram.

This is an incredibly cruel thing to do. Just think of the effect around trust on Isaac as he grows up! Imagine being a psychotherapist confronted with a life story like this! If Abraham did that today he would be in jail serving a long sentence. Some Christians somehow manage to see this story as a sign of God's 'love.' Love? Keep any of that 'God's love' stuff well away from me – pleeease!

Beat your slaves and have sex with the females:

If we are to believe the Bible, God supports slavery in both the Old and New Testaments. The Bible clearly approves of slavery and goes so far as to tell how to obtain slaves, how hard you can beat them, and when you can have sex with the female slaves!

Many Jews and Christians prefer to ignore the moral problems of slavery by saying that these slaves were actually servants or indentured servants. Many translations of the Bible use the word 'servant,' 'bond servant,' or 'man servant' instead of 'slave' to make the Bible seem less immoral than it really is. While many slaves may have worked as household servants, that doesn't mean they were not slaves who were bought, sold, and treated like livestock. The following passage shows that slaves are clearly property to be bought and sold:

However, you may purchase male or female slaves from among the foreigners who live among you. You may also purchase the children of such resident foreigners, including those who have been born in your land. You may treat them as your property, passing them on to your children as a permanent inheritance. You may treat your slaves like this, but the people of Israel, your relatives, must never be treated this way. (Leviticus 25:44-46 NLT)

Beating slaves is okay … to a point:

When a man strikes his male or female slave with a rod so hard that the slave dies under his hand, he shall be punished. If, however, the slave survives for a day or two, he is not to be punished, since the slave is his own property. (Exodus 21:20-21 NAB)

So that must be the origin of the saying: 'beaten within an inch of your life.'

Slavery approved of in the New Testament:

Slaves, obey your earthly masters with deep respect and fear. Serve them sincerely as you would serve Christ. (Ephesians 6:5 NLT)

Christians who are slaves should give their masters full respect so that the name of God and his teaching will not be shamed. If your master is a Christian, that is no excuse for being disrespectful. You should work all the harder because you are helping another believer by your efforts. Teach these truths, Timothy, and encourage everyone to obey them. (1Timothy 6:1-2 NLT)

Slaves, obey in everything those who are your earthly masters. (Colossians 3:22)

... bid slaves to be submissive to their masters and give satisfaction in every respect. (Titus 2:9)

The God of the New Testament commits murder:

'And the one seated upon it is called Faithful and True and he judges and carries on war in righteousness. His eyes are a fiery flame and upon his head are many diadems. He has a name written that no one knows except he himself. And he is arrayed with an outer garment sprinkled with blood and the name he is called is The Word of God Also the armies that were in heaven were following him on white horses, and they were clothed in white, clean fine linen. ***And out of his mouth there protrudes a sharp long sword that he may strike the nations with it and he will shepherd them with a rod of iron. He treads too the winepress of the wrath of God the Almighty.'*** (Revelation 19: 11 - 15)

'Any man that has disregarded the Law of Moses dies without compassion upon the testimony of two or three.' (Paul in Hebrews 10:28)

So it just takes two or three to rat on one person and they end up dead? Hebrews 10:29 is interesting too, but let us go on to 10:30-31:

'For we know him that said 'Vengeance is mine: I will recompense'; and again: 'Jehovah will judge his people. ***It is a fearful thing to fall into the hands of the living God.'***

And again: '... *I the Lord thy God am a* ***jealous God****, visiting the iniquity of the fathers upon the children unto the third and fourth generation.'* (Exodus 20:5)

~ ~ ~

A God of Love? No way: a god of fear, threat, rage, jealousy, murder, death and destruction. This god-chap sounds just like a devil. Funny, that. How is it so many people still, in this 21st century, when we presume lots of people to be intelligent, worship this ghastly, murderous, appalling, vengeful concept of a deity?

It wasn't always like this:

"War is a primary patriarchal contribution to culture, almost entirely absent from the matriarchal societies of the Neolithic and early Bronze ages. Even when Goddess-worshipping was beginning to give way to cults of aggressive gods, for along time the appearance of the Goddess imposed peace on all hostile groups. Among Germanic Tribes in Europe, Tacitus said, whenever the Goddess moved in her chariot at certain seasons to certain sacred places, the people 'do not go to battle or wear arms; every weapon is under lock; peace and quiet are known and welcomed'.... Patriarchal gods tended to be warlike from their inception – including, or even particularly the Judeo-Christian God.... Christianity was never a pacifist religion ... all-male Christianity was disseminated by violence."

— Barbara G.Walker, *Womens Enclyclopedia* (p.1058)

Well, so much for 'God' in His Own Words. I appeal to Christians – have you actually read the Bible? I mean *read* it – lots of it – intelligently – taking in what it actually says? And do you act on its instructions? Do you stone those who it says deserve it? Do you burn, murder, destroy according to the Bible's instructions? Why not? If this is the word of your God, why are you not obeying it? Oh, I see, you're just a 'convenience-Christian.' You take the nice bits and leave the rest. So you don't actually believe all the Bible at all, do you? I know you don't because if you did, you would be in jail for obeying its strictures.

~ ~ ~

So what about 'his son'? Let's hear from Jesus in some of his lesser known, not so nice words.

Jesus in His Own Words

There are a lot of beautiful words credited to Jesus in the Bible, many of which will be familiar. But there are others, too, which paint a challengingly different picture:

In Matthew 10:34, Jesus says:

"Don't imagine that I came to bring peace on earth! No, rather a sword. If you love your father, mother, sister, brother, more than me, you are not worthy of being mine."

Well, he certainly succeeded in that. Just look the peace stakes over the last two thousand years, culminating in the 20th century with two world wars and now enough weapons of mass destruction to destroy virtually all of us.

Brother shall deliver up the brother to death, and the father the child: and the children shall rise up against their parents, and cause them to be put to death. (Matthew 10:21)

Sounds like Russian Totalitarianism at its worst. Or the Inquisition – 600 years of imprisonment, murder and torture across Europe, courtesy the Roman Catholic Church.

Do not think I came to destroy the Law and the Prophets. I came not to destroy but to fulfill. (Matthew 5:17)

So Jesus approves of the Old Testament law and the prophets. He apparently supports the incredible cruelties of the Old Testament God as listed earlier.

Controversially in Luke 14:26-27, Jesus says: *"If any man come unto me, and hate not his father, and mother, and wife, and children, and brother, and sisters, yea, and his own life also, he can not be my disciple. Whoever is not carrying his torture stake and coming after me cannot be my disciple."*

Yet in Matthew 15:4, he says: *God said "Honor thy mother and father. Let him that reviles father or mother end up in death."*

Also see Ephesians 5:25: *'Husbands continue loving your wives, just as the Christ also loved the congregation and delivered himself up for it.'*

Matthew 10:34: *"I came not to send peace but a sword"*

Matthew 26:52: *"Put up again thy sword into his place: for all that take the sword shall perish with the sword".*

Another contradiction is in John 5:31: *"If I alone bear witness about myself, my witness is not true,"* while in John 8:14, we see: *"Even if I do bear witness of myself, my witness is true."*

In Luke 19:27, he says: *'But those mine enemies, which would not that I should reign over them, bring hither, and slay them before me.'*

And in Mark 16:16: *He that believeth and is baptized shall be saved; but he that believeth not* ***shall be damned.***

No messing, no choice, just believe as you're told and shut up!

… and from a distance he caught sight of a fig tree that had leaves and he went to see whether he would perhaps find something on it. But on coming on it, he found nothing but leaves, for it was not in the season of figs. So, in response, he said to it. "Let no one east fruit from you anymore forever." (Mark 11:13-14)

Jesus kills a fig tree for not bearing figs, even though it was out of season. You'd think the son of god would know that trees don't bear fruit in dry season.

Yet very differently he says, 'turn the other cheek,' do not react to violence with violence. This was a radically different teaching to the Jewish Torah (Old Testament) which, as you can see from the above god-statements, was a teaching of utmost reactive violence. Furthermore Jesus says: *'Behold, the kingdom of heaven is* ***within you.'***

So God is within, not outside you, and by implication, in the world, not outside it. This is the understanding of the heathens – god is in the heath, i.e., in nature. And nature includes people.

And now this most interesting of all the statements attributed to Jesus: *"Verily, verily, I say unto you, He that believeth in me, the works that I do shall he also; and greater works than these shall he do."*

Another translation says it fractionally differently: *'Most truly I say to you. He that exercises faith in me, that one will also do the works that I do; and he will do works greater than these, because I am going my way to the father."* (John 14:12)

This is a very interesting statement. It says if you exercise faith in Jesus / believe in Jesus, then you – or I – will be able to do what he can and even greater works than his, 'miracles' and all. That completely contradicts any idea that Jesus is super-special. He is saying that we can all achieve the same as him. How? By exercising faith in him or by believing in him. Just what does this really mean?

If you understand Jesus as the *eternal god-man / woman* within all of us, it makes complete sense. Whereas if you say you have to believe in just the one person, Jesus, who lived at one time 2,000 years ago, and every other religion and spiritual path is wrong (and everyone who lived before Jesus and who couldn't believe in him because he didn't exist is therefore left in 'limbo'), you end up in a world domination cult with some very crazy upside-down scriptures to 'prove' your case.

The ultimate point is that the Real God – Infinite Creator – creates all humans, all beings, all planets and stars and is The Creation.

WE ARE ALL SONS AND DAUGHTERS
OF THE REAL GOD.

~ ~ ~

Twenty five years ago, I took a class to learn metal bending by thought, Uri Geller style. The essence taught was that once you *really* believed you could, you could! And while you believed you couldn't, you couldn't! And the results bore that out.

Puts me in mind of the statement by Henry Ford, who demonstrated with Ford Motor Company that he was someone who knew he could – and did! "Whether you believe you can or whether you believe you can't, **you're right!**"

Here are a few more appropriate quotations from many sources.

"The world is as you dream it." — Numi, Equadorian shaman
"A man's life is what his thoughts make of it." — Marcus Aurelius
"As a man thinketh in his heart so is he." — Proverbs 23:7
"We are what we think, all that arises with our thoughts." — Buddha.
"You become what you think about." — Earl Nightingale
"The ancestor of every action is a thought." — Emerson
"With our thoughts we make the world." — Buddha.

So what is it we need to believe in? Our own ability, power; our Self as a 'Son/Daughter of God,' an integral part of the Whole, included, accepted, loved; able and authorized by right to tap into the Universal Power Source, the Real God.

Nelson Mandela, a person whose life demonstrates the actualization of the seemingly impossible, quoted a passage by Marianne Williamson from *A Return to Love: Reflections on the Principles of A Course In Miracles* in his inauguration speech which has become well known:

"Our deepest fear is not that we are inadequate. Our deepest fear is that we are powerful beyond measure. It is our light, not our darkness that most frightens us. We ask ourselves, Who am I to be brilliant, gorgeous, talented, fabulous? Actually, who are you not to be? You are a child of God. Your playing small does not serve the world. There is nothing enlightened about shrinking so that other people won't feel insecure around you. We are all meant to shine, as children do. We were born to make manifest the glory of God that is within us. It is not just in some of us; it is in everyone. And as we let our own light shine, we unconsciously give other people permission to do the same. As we are liberated from our own fear, our presence automatically liberates others."

So what is it we need to believe in or to have faith in that really brings the power to change things? What happens when 'faith' healers – or any healers – do work that works and that defies medical science? Some call on Jesus, some call on other deities, some are taken over by spirit doctors and some just do it. All of them have faith that *The Universal Power* will come through them and do the work. Almost none of them credit themselves with the power.

About 6 years ago, I had an interesting experience in the Philippines with a psychic healer and it was definitely a non-logical, beyond-the-rational time. Wearing a short-sleeved, open-necked shirt, he performed numerous operations on myself and my colleague with just the three of us present, while the other one of us acted as assistant. He would 'enter' the body lying on the table in his small treatment room – or hotel bed when we traveled to see some sights – and blood would appear and then he would pull 'stuff' out, innards of various kinds, bloody bits of matter. Just how much of it was very adept slight of hand (even though observed with eagle eyes from very close) and how much was 'real' in this dimension is still something I don't know to this day. But I do know it made a difference to me and my friend.

My colleague had suffered a near-fatal elevator crash 20 years earlier and had leftover knee and back problems. After sessions over two visits, about three weeks in all, his body shape is quite literally different, as is the way he walks and can use his body. I remember a moment when the healer pointed out to me a lump in his back. I felt it, a solid lump between the tendons in the upper back, which we all know can get very hard and knotted. He did an operation, very quickly, blood flowed, matter was brought out – and when I felt for the lump afterwards, I couldn't find it!

So many magical, non-logical healings are reported all over the world that it is a wonder to me that the majority still takes the world literally and thinks in purely materialistic terms.

One thing is for certain. Magical healing is not special to the realm of Jesus or any one individual or belief system. The power we need to believe in and have faith in is the Universal Power of All Creation.

Chapter 4

A Proper Religion?

"Not one of those modern, spiritual ideas cobbled together from many different sources. No, I want something properly established that has one source and one god and proper commandments that everyone agrees upon, something I can just believe in and leave it at that"

Well, let's look at some truth about how the Christian religion came together to become what it is. Christianity as we know it was founded by the Emperor Constantine and became effectively formalized into an arm of the state in AD325 at the Council of Nicaea.

Flavius Valerius Constantius (c. 285-337 AD), Constantine the Great, was the son of Emperor Constantius I. When his father died in 306 AD, Constantine became emperor of Britain, Gaul (now France), and Spain. Gradually he gained control of the entire Roman Empire.

It seems that in 312 AD, Constantine responded to a dream by converting from Paganism to Christianity so that, all of a sudden, it was good to be Christian and bad to be a Pagan. Within a century of Constantine's conversion, the Empire went from roughly ten percent Christian (most of these believing in now extinct "heretical" Christianities) to mostly Roman Christian. How did the conversion happen? Partly by giving Christians preference for government contracts and advancement! (Sounds familiar!) Also by some serious coercion:

"Constantine made divination in public matters punishable by burning to death. Pagan sacrifices were banned in 341 AD, and nocturnal pagan worship was forbidden in 353 AD. By mid-century, pagan temples were ordered closed, and in 356 AD, worship of non-Christian images became a capital crime."
— POCM - Pagan Origins of the Christ Myth – see www. medmalexperts. com/POCM/index.html.

Theological differences regarding just who Jesus Christ was began to manifest in Constantine's empire when two major opponents surfaced and argued virulently whether Jesus Christ was a created being (Arius doctrine) or not created but rather co-equal and co-eternal to God his father (Athanasius doctrine).

It seems the theological warfare between the Arius and Athanasius camps became intense. Constantine realized his empire was being threatened by this doctrinal rift and pressured the church to sort out its differences before the results created a massive split. Finally the emperor called a council at Nicaea in 325 AD to resolve the dispute.

Only a fraction of existing bishops, 318, attended, or about 18% of all the bishops in the empire. Of the 318, approximately 10 were from the Western part of Constantine's empire, making the voting lopsided at best. The emperor manipulated, coerced and threatened the council to be sure it voted for what he wanted rather than an actual consensus of the bishops.

The present day Christian Church calls Constantine the first Christian emperor; however, his 'Christianity' was nothing but politically motivated. He had been a follower of Mithras, an earlier Middle-Eastern 'god-man' story from Persia, very similar to that of Jesus. (We will look more deeply at Mithras in chapter 5.) Whether he ever personally accepted Christian doctrine is more than doubtful. He had one of his sons murdered in addition to a nephew, his brother-in-law and probably one of his wives – not ideal Christian behavior. Apparently he continued to retain his title of high priest in the Mithraic religion until his death, and was not baptized into Christianity until he was on his deathbed.

The majority of bishops voted under pressure from Constantine for the Athanasius doctrine, so a creed was adopted that favored Athanasius' theology, and Arius was condemned and exiled. Several of the bishops left before the voting to avoid the controversy. Jesus Christ was approved to be "one substance" with God the Father. It is interesting that, even today, the Eastern and Western Orthodox churches disagree with each other regarding this doctrine.

Two of the bishops who voted pro-Arius were also exiled and Arius' writings were destroyed. Constantine decreed that anyone caught with Arius documents would be subject to the death penalty. A good loving Christian response? Well, it would fit with the Inquisition over a thousand years later, but it is not really quite the idea supposedly promoted by Jesus. It is, however, very typical of emperors and Church power brokers.

Here is the Nicene Creed as formulated by the Athenasius teachings:

We believe in one God,
the Father, the Almighty,
maker of heaven and earth,
of all that is, seen and unseen.
We believe in one Lord, Jesus Christ,
the only Son of God,
eternally begotten of the Father,
God from God, Light from Light,
true God from true God,
begotten, not made,

of one Being with the Father;
through him all things were made.
For us and for our salvation
he came down from heaven,
was incarnate of the Holy Spirit and the Virgin Mary
and became truly human.
For our sake he was crucified under Pontius Pilate;
he suffered death and was buried.
On the third day he rose again
in accordance with the Scriptures;
he ascended into heaven
and is seated at the right hand of the Father.
He will come again in glory to judge the living and the dead,
and his kingdom will have no end.
We believe in the Holy Spirit, the Lord, the giver of life,
who proceeds from the Father and the Son,
who with the Father and the Son is worshiped and glorified,
who has spoken through the prophets.
We believe in one holy catholic and apostolic Church.
We acknowledge one baptism for the forgiveness of sins.
We look for the resurrection of the dead,
and the life of the world to come. Amen.

Well, there's no messing about with what we are all supposed to believe. Especially in one Holy Apostolic Church – no messing where the power is intended to lie. It's worth remembering that disagreeing with an emperor (or his appointed church) is a dodgy business. You can ever so easily find your life is forfeit, so the pressure to agree, whatever you might privately think, is seriously large.

Today we call that *mind control* or *totalitarianism.*

Even with the adoption of the Nicaean Creed, it seems that problems continued and after a few years, the Arian faction began to regain control. In fact, they became so powerful that Constantine restored them and denounced the Athanasius group! Well, it seems public pressure did impress the emperor and he bent to their power – and annexed it to his. He ended Arius' exile along with the bishops who sided with him. And now he banished Athanasius and his followers!

Reminds me of Queens Mary and Elizabeth and Catholic vs Protestant killings about 1200 years later. Get caught believing the wrong Christian religion at the wrong time and you suddenly find yourself very dead. Same with Islam as they gear up for another war between Sunnis and Shias.

When Constantine died (after being baptized by an Arian bishop), his son fully reinstated the Arian philosophy and bishops, and enforced the condemnation of the Athanasius group. In the following years, the political foes continued to struggle and finally the Arians were overthrown and Athenasius reinstated! Up, down and roundabout – and this is 'one true religion'? This controversy caused widespread bloodshed and killing.

In 381 AD, Emperor Theodosius who favored the Trinitarian ideas of Athanasius convened a council in Constantinople. Only Trinitarian bishops were invited to attend. 150 bishops attended and voted to alter the Nicene Creed to include the Holy Spirit as a part of the Godhead. The Trinity doctrine then became official for both the church and the state. Dissident bishops were expelled from the church and excommunicated. Same old jazz – never mind actual beliefs or convictions, just watch out or you'll suddenly find the wind blowing the other way with you on the wrong side.

The Athanasius Trinitarian Creed was finally established in probably the 5th century. It was not written by Athanasius but adopted his name. It stated in part:

"We worship one God in Trinity . . . The Father is God, the Son is God, and the Holy Ghost is God; and yet they are not three gods, but one God."

I guess they didn't major in mathematics. $1 + 1 + 1 = 1$. Well, if the emperor says so, then it must be so.

By the 9th century, the creed was established in Spain, France and Germany. It had taken centuries for the trinity doctrine to be accepted, and I wonder how much coercion and political pressure and threats it took. It was only because of church and government politics that the trinity came into existence at all and became church orthodoxy.

Here is the current version of the creed as mainly in use today:

I believe in God, the Father Almighty,
the Creator of heaven and earth,
and in Jesus Christ, His only Son, our Lord:
Who was conceived of the Holy Spirit,
born of the Virgin Mary,
suffered under Pontius Pilate,
was crucified, died, and was buried.
He descended into hell.
The third day He arose again from the dead.
He ascended into heaven
and sits at the right hand of God the Father Almighty,
whence He shall come to judge the living and the dead.
I believe in the Holy Spirit, the holy catholic church,
the communion of saints,
the forgiveness of sins,
the resurrection of the body,
and life everlasting.
Amen.

It is good to remember that the Trinitarian Doctrine came from deceit, underhanded politics, a power hungry emperor and warring factions who brought about death and bloodshed to each other. Oh, and in 391, Theodosius outlawed all religions except Christianity. So much for choice.

Another false claim of the church is the doctrine of Apostolic Succession. The Church is known to have copied this idea from a Gnostic sect in the fourth century, and then fabricated lines of apostolic succession for the missing centuries. Very clever when you consider that the apostles they purport to succeed didn't exist anyway (as we'll see in the next chapter).

So much for 'one true religion' and 'one true church.'

(If it's not enough for you, read: *The Christ Conspiracy / The Dark Side of Christian history / The Jesus Mysteries / Jesus and the (lost) Goddess / The Laughing Jesus / The Woman's Encyclopedia of Myths and Secrets*. See Resources at end of this book.)

I remember at school chapel services repeating parrot fashion the Nicaean Creed, the cornerstone of Christianity. I repeated it without knowing what it really meant. Like so many, I was a 'Christian' because I'd always been told I was a Christian. I didn't understand the Creed but I knew it meant I was a bad person because there was no way I could live up to it or ever be good enough for this god-chap. I was a religious failure and therefore a personal failure and would always be so, and god had nothing much good for me except pain and hellishness. And the Great British Public School I attended certainly made sure every day contained its portion of suffering, thus proving again and again my utter lack of worth in the eyes of both God and his representatives, the human religious authorities, which included the schoolmasters and prefects. The education system certainly took up the punishment theme of Christianity to the full, as the use of cane, birch and other torture instruments was 'normal' right up to the 1970s in England. (The movie *If...* (1969) showed a graphic and accurate portrayal of the 'joys' of corporal punishment, public school style.)

At the 'Great British Public Schools' – so imitated around the Christian world and often run by religious groups – much flagellation was done by masters and much was handed over to the boy prefects who were armed with fearsome canes two-to-three feet long and the power to beat on the backside those they chose, for the most pettifogging and contrived reasons. That, folks, means 17- to 18-year-old boys with full 'god' and schoolmaster-given permission to attack the backsides of 13- to 16-year old boys who were supposed to bend over, present their rears and 'take it like a man.' Marquis de Sade, did you get your first experiences in one of these establishments? One thing is for sure, the dominatrixes of Great Britain, and probably much of Christianized Europe and America, have been kept busy for centuries by the ex-pupils of these 'great' establishments reliving their schooldays.

Here is the god-chap supporting the brutalization of young boys:

He that spareth the rod, hateth his son. (Proverbs 13:24)

Withhold not correction from the child: for if thou beatest him with the rod, he shall not die. Thou shalt beat him with the rod, and shalt deliver his soul from hell. (Proverbs 23:13-14)

I wonder how many schoolmasters through the ages have thanked 'god' regularly for such biblical injunctions to enable them to 'righteously' enjoy themselves at the expense of those unfortunates entrusted to their 'care.' Brutalized boys grow into brutal men, though the ones brutalized 'righteously' and 'for their own good' in the boarding school system tend to become men who live in deep denial of their true feelings and their true nature. And, with their memory semi-erased and their emotional life truncated, they happily send their sons to such boarding schools so they can be flagellated into the 'right kind of man' too. And all 'FOR THEIR OWN GOOD,' of course. (See *THE MAKING OF THEM* by Nick Duffell.)

Here is Mark Twain reflecting on his boyhood:

"The mind that becomes soiled in youth can never again be washed clean. I know this by my own experience, and to this day I cherish an unappeasable bitterness against the unfaithful guardians of my young life, who not only permitted but compelled me to read an unexpurgated Bible through before I was fifteen years old. None can do that and ever draw a clean, sweet breath again this side of the grave."

When it comes to religious flagellation, the 14th century Saint Catherine of Siena, it is said, whipped herself three times every day; once for her own sins, once for the sins of others, and once for the sins of the world. The 11th century zealot Dominicus Loricatus once repeated the entire Psalter (a collection of the psalms and other 'inspirational' material) twenty times in one week, accompanying each psalm with a hundred lash-strokes to his back. Members of Opus Dei wear a nasty buckle of spikes strapped on their thighs to keep them in constant pain ….

Well, whatever turns you on … or off.

The Nicaean Creed, far from being some great God-inspired treatise of truth, was cobbled together after bitter arguments and blows between factions of 318 bishops, and voted in by a small majority, under great pressure from the Emperor Constantine who demanded that they come to unity or suffer dire consequences. In following years, it was changed and changed again to suit the politics of those in the favor of the then emperor. Let us look at that incredible document now with more ancient eyes.

Looking way back to the old world before male-dominated religions, from an Earth-based culture's view, it makes no sense whatsoever to believe in what you don't know. If you take on a belief as a dogma without actually knowing by experience, how can you ever come to actually 'know' anything? The ancients studied nature and learned through experience. If they received a spiritual revelation, they would test it out and see if it worked before accepting it as a belief. The real adventure of life is to find out about life, to explore the Universe and how it works, to come to know more of the Great Mystery that is Existence, and to live a balanced, caring-sharing life as part of your community.

The Creed says one must believe in Jesus Christ as the only begotten son of God. If the rest of us humans are not begotten of God, surely there must be a far more powerful deity who has given birth to trillions and trillions of humans over a vast sea of time, to say nothing of all the animals, plants, planets and suns of the manifest Universe? Yes, there is!

The Creed says we must believe that Jesus is made of the same substance as the Father and therefore not the same as us mere humans. Therefore he had to be born of a virgin through a path other than the dreaded sex. That was fine until it was realized that if his mother was born through sex, the image was rather blown. His mother then also had to be born of a virgin. History doesn't record (as far as I know) whether they got to his grandmother – and great-grandmother – to make them virginally born too.

We are told to believe that Jesus, 'the only son of god' came to earth as a human and will return to sit in judgment over the rest of us. We all are supposed to live up to his impossible ideal or be judged wanting. What a great way to frighten people into self-rejection and submission. Bang goes self-worth and love and care for yourself. Jesus is reported to have said '*Love your neighbor as yourself.*' Wonderful sentiment but something went wrong in the yourself bit. Loving yourself has largely become equated with debauchery, sin and greed. I know what ribaldry and put-downs I will get in most circumstances if I declare that I love myself. Just imagine saying that to acquaintances in the pub!

We are told that only through Jesus can we get to heaven and a reasonable afterlife. Jesus is the only doorway into a heavenly future. So at a stroke, all other paths, everybody else's spirituality, are condemned as useless, and so it then becomes a Christian's 'duty' to convert everyone else ... or conquer them, kill them, eliminate their 'godless' culture and take their lands 'in the name of god.' How convenient for an emperor-dictator-murderer such as Constantine and later emperors and popes.

Here is an extract on the subject of murder and torture from *The Christ Conspiracy* by Acharya S (p.10):

"... Christian proponents had the right to purge the earth of 'evil' and to convert the 'heathen' to the 'true faith.' Over a period of more than a millennium, the Church would bring to bear in this 'purification' and 'conversion' to the religion of the 'Prince of Peace' the most horrendous torture methods ever devised, in the end slaughtering tens of millions worldwide.

"These 'conversion' methods by Catholics against men, women and children, Christians and Pagans alike, included burning, hanging and torture of all manner, using the tools described in Fourth Maccabees. Women and girls had hot pokers and sharp objects slammed up their vaginas, often after priests had raped them. Men and boys had their penises and testicles crushed or ripped or cut off. Both genders and all ages had their skin pulled off with hot pincers and their tongues ripped out, and were subjected to diabolical machinery designed for the weakest parts of the body, such as knees, ankles, elbows and fingertips, all of which were crushed. Their legs and arms were broken with sledgehammers, and, if there was anything left of them, they were hanged or burned alive. Nothing more evil could possibly be imagined, and from this absolute evil came the 'rapid' spread of Christianity.

"So far this despicable legacy and crime against humanity remains unavenged and its main culprit unpunished, not only standing intact but inexplicably receiving the undying and unthinking support of hundreds of millions.... This acquiescence is the result of the centuries of destruction and degradation of their ancestors' cultures, which demoralized them and ripped away their spirituality and heritage."

Horrendous. Even I have nothing to add to that!

And isn't it something that 'gentle Jesus' who, like Buddha, advocated poverty and humility, eventually became the mythic figurehead for one of the world's pre-eminent money-making organizations. The cynical Pope Leo X exclaimed, *"What profit has not that fable of Christ brought us!"*

— Barbara G. Walker. 'The Woman's Encyclopedia' (p471)

The blunt fact is that 'Jesus Christ' actually had little discernable effect on history at all. He was merely a pawn in the Roman control of much of the world. Before Jesus, Rome was the dominant controller empire of the world. After the empire collapsed, it was replaced by domination and control through the Roman Church with 'Jesus' on the cross as the figure for the mind-controlling, spirit-numbing concepts of original sin and guilt. One method of power and control was simply replaced by another. And, my 'God,' hasn't it been successful, just look at how many millions are still in-the-lie today!

IT'S TIME TO WAKE UP.

Here is an interesting current oddity. It seems Anglican clergy must *still* swear to agree to the so-called 'Thirty-nine Articles of Faith' set by Elizabeth 1 and her parliament, and which all citizens had to believe or else be condemned as heretics (which virtually amounted to a death sentence). It starts with the usual all-male suspects:

God consists of three persons, the father, the son, and Holy Ghost.

Later, however, there are some really interesting edicts like these:

All deserve God's wrath and damnation, but there is no condemnation of believers who are baptized.

Wow, look at that! Woe betide any poor sod who is not baptized, and if you don't believe what you are ordered to, you'd better keep your mouth well shut! Then we get this:

Predestination to life is the everlasting purpose of God, to deliver from curse and damnation those whom he has chosen in Christ, to bring them everlasting salvation.

So the god-chap first curses everybody and then chooses some to be saved?

Heyeokah says: God save us from 'god'!

Lastly here is another piece which is great for lazy people:

Our righteousness before God comes, not by our works, but by the merit of Christ. Therefore we are justified only by faith and not by works.

Just believe what you are told and all will be OK. Never mind action, never mind soiling yourself with work, never mind actually doing things for other people; just believe the 'right beliefs' and the god-chap will look after you. Really!

The separation and competition between Christian groups has gone on over the centuries and is still alive and well today. Here is Pat Robertson, the American TV evangelist, quoted in '700 Club,' 1991: "You say you're supposed to be nice to the Episcopalians and the Presbyterians and the Methodists, and this and that and the other thing. Nonsense, I don't have to be nice to the spirit of the Anti-Christ. I can love the people who hold false opinions, but I don't have to be nice to them."

The 'Devil'

So far, we haven't much mentioned this other chap who is supposedly so important in religion and has such a big part to play and so much to say for himself. I refer, of course, to the 'devil.' Perhaps I could say 'devil-chap' as from the religionists' point of view, he is all-male, too. If we take the Bible seriously, the god-chap has constant trouble with the devil-chap by whom he is only too frequently outwitted.

If we go back to older cultures, we find no devil but instead representative figures of human egotism and stupidity such as 'Coyote,' the Native American trickster figure, and Mulla Nasrudin, the Indian comic figure who screws up all over the place. The real God, the Infinite-Creator includes all that religions call devil/evil. In fact, by making their God all good, they miss the way creation works completely (see Chapter 7). And remember, Lucifer is the light-bringer, which means without Lucifer we have no light!

In religion's world, the god-chap is always on both sides in a war as both sides pray to the same god-chap. One wins and says, "God delivered mine enemies to me," and the other loses and asks, "What have I done for god to desert me in this way?" Or perhaps bemoans the idea that the devil was somehow stronger. Creation includes all; earthquakes happen and people get hurt, volcanoes erupt and whole towns get swept away. That's just the way it is. But good and evil are what we humans do, Creation just does its thing! In the words of Sufi poet Rumi (1207-1273):

'Out beyond ideas of
right-doing and wrong-doing
there is a field.
I'll meet you there'

To further explore the history of God-Men, we need to go back to much earlier times. Long before the time of Jesus, the myth of the God-Man existed in many countries of the world ....

Chapter 5

The Many God-Men Before Jesus

"When we say that the Word, who is the first-birth of God, was produced without sexual union, and that He, Jesus Christ, our Teacher, was crucified and died, and rose again, and ascended into heaven, we propounded nothing different from what you believe regarding those whom you esteem sons of Jupiter"

— Justin Martyr, First apology, 21

In other words, it is the same in essence as the Pagan beliefs before Christianity. One thing is certain – far from being the first, Jesus was the last of a long line of God-Men and his story had been told many times before in many cultures.

Horus

Consider Horus. Heard of him? No? Well, if you are or have been a Christian, you've heard his story many times:

- Horus, like Jesus, was the "only begotten son of God." In this case, God was called Osiris.
- Horus's mother was MERI. Jesus' mother was MARY.
- The foster father of Horus was Seb.
- The foster father of Jesus was Joseph. Both of them were of 'royal descent.'

- Isis-Meri conceived Horus without the "seed of the living father." Osiris was both *dead* and had no penis, so Isis-Meri made a dildo out of clay. Mary conceived Jesus without the seed of a living father.
- Horus was born 'in a cave'; Jesus was born 'in a stable.'
- Horus was heralded by the star Sirius and witnessed by '3 solar deities.' Jesus was heralded by 'a Star in the East.' Sirius just so happens to be the brightest star in the East that rises at dawn. The Three Wise Men are the 3 stars on Orion's Belt. The title of these stars for thousands of years was 'The Three Kings of Orion.'
- Horus's birth date was at the time of the winter solstice (December 21-22) with December 25 being the date the SUN begins to 'rise again' as it is the first day that is measurably longer. Jesus' birth date is recognized as December 25, the same date as the birthday of Mithras, Dionysus and the Sol Invictus (unconquerable Sun), and many other God-men of ancient mythology.
- Herut tried to have Horus murdered. Herod tried to have Jesus murdered.
- God tells Horus' mother, "Come, thou goddess Isis-Meri, hide thyself with thy child." An angel tells Jesus' father to: "Arise and take the young child and his mother and flee into Egypt."
- Horus came of age (12) with a special ritual when his eye was restored. Jesus was taken by parents to the temple for what is today called a Bar Mitzvah ritual, his age? 12. This is when they both 'came of age.'
- Jesus reputedly challenged the elders of the temple at this age. Just as every adolescent challenges the status quo!
- Between the ages of 12-30, there is nothing written about either Horus or Jesus.
- Horus was baptized in the river Eridanus. There is a Constellation called Eridanus that looks like a river in the sky. Jesus was baptized in the river Jordan.

- Horus was baptized by Anup the Baptizer." Jesus was baptized by John the Baptist. Both baptizers were beheaded.
- Jesus & Horus went through temptations at the same period in their lives. Horus was taken from the desert of Amenta up a high mountain by his arch-rival Sut. (Sut or Set-An was a precursor for the Hebrew Satan.) Jesus was taken from the desert in Palestine up a high mountain by his arch-rival Satan.
- Horus walked on water, cast out demons, healed the sick, restored sight to the blind. He 'stilled the sea by his power.' Jesus walked on water, cast out demons, healed the sick, restored sight to the blind. He stilled the sea with the command: "Peace, be still".
- The place of resurrection for Horus was Anu, an Egyptian city where the rites of the death, burial and resurrection of Horus were enacted annually. The place of resurrection for Jesus was Bethany. Hebrews added their prefix for house (beth) to Anu to produce 'Beth-Anu,' or the House of Anu. Since 'u' and 'y' were interchangeable in antiquity, Bethanu became Bethany.
- Horus raised Asar from the dead. He was referred to as 'the Asar,' as a sign of respect. Translated into Hebrew, this is El-Asar. The Romans added the suffix 'us' to indicate a male name, producing Elasarus.' Over time, the 'E' was dropped and 's' became 'z,' producing the name Lazarus.
- Horus was 'the Lamb'; Jesus was 'the Lamb.'
- Horus was 'the way, the truth and the life,' by name and in person. Jesus was 'the way, the truth and the life.'
- Horus is the Good Shepherd with the crook upon his shoulders. Jesus was the Good Shepherd with the lamb upon his shoulders.
- Horus and Jesus both had 12 Disciples. Once we drop the literalist myth, we can dare to realize these are SUN

> of God myths, we can see that the disciples are the 12 houses of the zodiac.

And by the way, the Horus story dates back a thousand years or more before Jesus. The very idea that Jesus is the literal 'only son of God' and that his story is in any way unique is ridiculous and easily dumped through a proper in-depth look at historical records. No wonder there are so many injunctions for Christians to read nothing but the Bible – they might learn too much to remain Christians!

There are many such *God-men, saviors, Messiahs, Sons of God*, all of whom pre-date Jesus. Here are a few more:

Attis

The worship of Attis and Cybele dates back centuries in Phrygia (modern Turkey) and it was imported to Rome in 204 BC. Roman writers mentioning the religion include: Lucretius (98 - 54 BC), Catullus (86 - 40 BC), Varro (116 - 28 BC), and Dionysus Halicarnasensis (first century BC). The 'Festival of Joy' which celebrated Attis' death and rebirth was a yearly event in Rome before and during the years the Christian Gospels were written (from the reign of Claudius, 41 - 54 AD).

"On March 22 a pine tree was brought to the sanctuary of Cybele, on it hung the effigy of Attis. The God was dead. Two days of mourning followed, but when night fell on the eve of the third day, the worshippers turned to joy. 'For suddenly a light shone in the darkness; the tomb was opened; the God had risen from the dead … [and the priest] softly whispered in their ears the glad tidings of salvation. The resurrection of the God was hailed by his disciples as a promise that they too would issue triumphant from the corruption of the grave.'"

— Frazer, *Attis*, chapter 1

The worshippers of Attis then ate a sacramental meal of bread and wine. The wine represented the God's blood; the bread became the body of the savior.

Baptism was a serious ceremony: a bull was placed over a grating and the devotee stood under the grating. The bull was then stabbed with a consecrated spear and, "Its hot reeking blood poured in torrents through the apertures and was received with devout eagerness by the worshipper … who had been born again to eternal life and had washed away his sins in the blood of the bull."

Heavy duty when you compare it with modern day church wine and biscuit!

The basics of the Attis story were:

- He was born of the virgin Nana on December 25.
- He was both the divine father and the divine son.
- He was a savior who was crucified in a tree for the salvation of mankind and was buried, but on the third day the priests found the tomb empty as he had arisen from the dead. The date was March 25.
- His followers were baptized in blood, thereby washing away their sins, after which they were declared '*born again*.'
- His followers ate a sacred meal of bread which they believed became the body of the savior.
- At the spring solstice celebration, he is depicted hanging on a tree.
- He is called 'The Good Shepherd,' the 'Most High God,' the 'Only Begotten Son,' and the 'Savior.'

Mithras

Here is another pre-Jesus God-man myth:

- Mithras was born in a cave, on December 25, of a virgin mother. He came from heaven to be born as a man, to redeem men from their sin. He was known as Savior, Son of God, Redeemer, and Lamb of God.

- Every year at the first minute of December 25, the temple of Mithras was lit with candles and priests in white garments *celebrated the birth of the Son of God.*
- His followers kept the Sabbath holy, eating sacramental meals in remembrance of Him. The sacred meal of bread and water, or bread and wine, was symbolic of the body and blood of the sacred bull.
- Mithraic rituals were to bring about the transformation and salvation of His adherents – the ascent of the soul to the realm of the divine. On the wall of a Mithraic temple in Rome is the inscription: "And thou hast saved us by shedding the eternal blood."
- The great Mithraic festivals celebrated his birth (at the winter solstice) and his death and resurrection (at the spring solstice).

The Devil's Mimicry!

A Christian writer of the fourth century AD recounted ongoing disputes between Pagans and Christians over the remarkable similarities of the death and resurrection of their gods. The Pagans argued that their Gods were older and therefore original. The Christians admitted Christ came later, but claimed Attis / Mithras was a work of the devil and their similarity to Christ, and the fact they predated Christ, were intended to confuse and mislead men.

Now isn't that just great. But there is one problem – well a lot really, but let us just look at one. If the 'devil' is so clever as to create the Jesus story long before 'god,' doesn't that make the 'devil' seriously prescient and 'god' a bit of a dimwit?

Here is a recent Creationist Christian creating a wonderful story, Monty Pythonesque in its fabulous implausablility. He says that before the Great Flood and the time of Noah, there were good and bad angels/demons who had come down to earth in disobedience of God and that when the flood wiped out almost all mankind, it didn't kill the bad angels and so they lived for many years without people around to see what they got up to. So during that time, Satan, their leader got them to make up fake fossils and dinosaur bones and bury them all over the place to trick later generations of people into thinking history was longer than what the Bible and the good Bishop Ussher decreed. Well, at least you have to give the fool credit for sheer creative invention!

Buddha

Let us look at some more of the many God-Men who preceded Jesus and carried the same myth, starting with Buddha:

- He was born of the **Virgin Maya (!)** on December 25, announced by a star and attended by wise men presenting costly gifts. At his birth angels sang heavenly songs.
- He taught in temple at age 12.
- He was tempted by Mara, the Evil One, while fasting.
- He was baptized in water with the Spirit of God present.
- He healed the sick, fed 500 from a small basket of cakes, walked on water.
- He came to fulfill the law and preached the establishment of a kingdom of righteousness.
- He taught that his followers should renounce the world and embrace a life of poverty.
- He was transfigured on a mount.
- He died (on a cross, in some traditions), was buried but rose again after the tomb was opened by supernatural powers.
- He ascended into heaven (Nirvana) and will return in later days to judge the dead.
- He was called: Good Shepherd, Carpenter, Alpha and Omega, Sin Bearer, Master, Light of the World, Redeemer, etc.

Notice anything similar?

There have been many Buddhas over the centuries up to the last one about 2,500 years ago. They are no more corporeal than Jesus or any of the other God-men.

Dionysos / Bacchus

Here is Dionysos, also known as Bacchus, the Greek version of the myth. The essence of the Dionysos story is:

- Born of a virgin on December 25 and placed in a manger.
- He became a traveling teacher and performed many miracles.
- He rode in a triumphal procession on an ass.
- He turned water into wine.
- His followers ate a sacred meal that became the body of the God.
- He rose from the dead on March 25.
- He was identified with the ram and the lamb.
- Called: King of Kings, Only Begotten Son, Savior, Redeemer, Sin-bearer, Anointed One, and the Alpha and Omega.

Virishna

And another! Here is the story of Virishna, a heathen savior said to date back to 1200 BC.

Incidentally, do you know the meaning of *heathen*, so derided by Christians? A heathen (me) is one *who sees God in the heath*, i.e., in nature, in everything. And where else would you look? If God is not in the substance of life, of existence – and the very substance of life/existence in God – then where is S/He?

Virishna was immaculately conceived and born of a spotless virgin who had 'never known man' and who was impregnated by a spirit. Angels and shepherds attended his birth offering frankincense and myrrh. His birth occurred according to a prophecy; he was threatened in early life by the local tyrant Cansa and his parents fled with him to Gokul. All the male children under two were then murdered by Cansa. He was saluted and worshipped as the 'savior of men'; he led a life of humility and service, wrought astounding miracles including healing the sick, restoring sight to the blind, casting out devils, raising the dead, etc. He was put to death on a cross between two thieves. He descended to hell, rose from the dead and ascended up to heaven 'in the sight of all men.'

Well, you can hardly get closer than that!

There are an awful lot of God-Men in mythology and here is a list, courtesy of *The Book Your Church Does Not Want You to Read.* (But please do, it is a good read! p.135):

- Krishna of Hindostan
- Buddha Sakia of India
- Salivahana of Bermuda
- Osiris of Egypt
- Horus of Egypt
- Odin of Scandinavia
- Crite of Chaldea
- Zoroaster of Persia
- Mithra – also Persia
- Baal and Taut of Phoenicia
- Indra of Tibet
- Bali of Afghanistan
- Jao of Nepal
- Virishna - circa 1200 BC
- Wittoba of the Bilingonese
- Thammuz of Syria
- Attis of Phrigia
- Xamolxis of Thrace
- Zoar of the Bonzes

- Adad of Assyria
- Deva Tat and Sammonocadam of Siam
- Alcides of Thebes
- Mikado of the Sintoos
- Beddru of Japan
- Hesus or Eros, and Bremrillah of the Druids
- Thor, son of Odin, of the Gauls
- Cadmus of Greece
- Dionysos, also Greece
- Adonis, son of the virgin Io of Greece
- Hil and Feta of the Mandaites
- Quetzalcoatl of Mexico. Also Gentaut.
- Prometheus of Caucasus
- Ischy of Formosa
- Fohi and Tien of China
- Ixion nd Quirinus of Rome
- Mohamud, or Mahomet, of Arabia

Some say the myth of the dying-reborn god probably started in Asia Minor, although it could well be more universal because we find it in Mexico around 300 BC in the myth of Quetzalcoatl and as far east as China. The ancient Greeks and Romans inherited and adapted gods from places like Assyria, Babylon, Phrygia, Persia, Mesopotamia and Egypt. The ancient religions were about the cycles of the Sun (the Sun of God) and the Earth (The Divine Mother) and the cycles of nature. They saw the great forces of the Universe as 'gods' who personified nature's cycles by dying in the autumn and being reborn in the spring.

All the evidence shows quite conclusively that a gigantic fraud of monumental proportions has been perpetrated upon us. Jesus Christ is a story and never was a person. Here is Archarya S writing in *The Christ Conspiracy:*

"The fact is that this crowd-drawing preacher finds his place in 'history' only in the New Testament, **completely overlooked**

by the dozens of historians of his day, an era considered one of the best documented in history."

And Albert Schweitzer in his book *The Quest for the Historical Jesus* wrote:

"There is nothing more negative than the result of the critical study of the life of Jesus … it has fallen to pieces, cleft and disintegrated by the concrete historical problems which came to the surface one after another." (Quoted in *The Laughing Jesus* by Timothy Freke and Peter Gandy, p.60.)

Now it is time for us to honor the cycles of nature once again. To honor the true SUN OF GOD as that giant powerful being in the sky upon whom we *totally* depend for our existence and to honor the Virgin Mary, Mare, Isis, Eve, The Divine Mother, our planet, the Earth upon whom we totally depend for our material existence. We are trashing Our Mother and unless we change our ways quite dramatically, there is every reason to suppose she will not be able to provide for us and we, those who survive, will be forced to change our ways and to think again who we are and why we are here.

And this means worshipping different 'gods,' gods who are in tune with nature and who guide us to live in harmony with our planet and her cycles.

It means growing up out of eternally fighting each other. Learning to live in harmony and love instead of hate, war and strife.

IT IS GROW-UP-OR-DIE TIME, FOLKS.

This myth is about all of us. We are the god-wo/men of these myths.

We are all born of the Holy Spirit, the ineffable consciousness that is in everything. We are all born into matter on planet Earth, our true mother, the 'Virgin Mare' – the ocean. All life begins in the sea. Or we can express it as the 'Virgin Mater'

(Latin) = Mother = matter. We are born from spirit into substance to experience life on earth.

We all suffer in this life of limitation on the 'cross' of restriction – the cross of earth, air, water and fire – or more specifically, body, mind, emotions, and spirit. We all naturally challenge our elders and the status quo at or around the age of 12 when puberty begins. We all spend time working and making a career in an ordinary job. We are all 'tempted by the devil' to lie, cheat, indulge and take the easy way at others' expense. We are all challenged at some stage by life (God) to *die to our egoism so we can be reborn to spirit-consciousness = awakened to our true nature as part of All-Creation.* If we manage to achieve that honorable and divine state (a gigantic task), we become a 'person of knowledge' and a wise elder and teacher to the younger, who can lead and guide the people to a healthy and sustainable life.

Now you may have noticed, there are not a lot of wise elders around. Why? Because the real teaching of this wonderful myth has been subverted into a warlike, male-dominated, dogmatic belief system that offers a false 'heaven' as a reward if you do as you're told, think as you're told, believe as you're told, live as you're told, and don't rock any boats. So those who might have become our elders became 'old people' with little or nothing to offer. They have been brainwashed. Many end up segregated in homes. Shame.

More than shame. It still happens to us, too, in present time. This needs to change. Our very survival is at stake and the survival of future generations even more so. Unless we change, unless we grow up and take responsibility, they will look back on us as a deluded bunch of deeply selfish, ignorant pigs who trashed their planet and their future.

IT'S TIME TO WAKE UP!

Chapter 6

'God' Hates Sex, Women and Human Bodies

Let's start with sex and marriage. The Bible says marriage shall be "between one man and one or more women." In Genesis 29:17-35, Jacob works seven years for Rachel and gets Leah substituted and then gets Rachel as well!

Samuel 2: 5-13: *"and David went on taking more concubines and wives."*

Well, the Bible is the word of God, that's what they say, so it must be okay. Just feel a bit sad I rather missed out on concubines in this lifetime. Missed out like – er – totally.

1Kings 11:3 says of Solomon: *"And he came to have seven hundred wives, princesses and three hundred concubines."*

Seems I missed out on 699 other wives, too.

How about 2Chronicles: 11-21. *"And Reho-boam was more in love with Ma'a'cah, the granddaughter of Absolom than all his other wives that he had taken and his concubines, for there were eighteen wives he had taken, also sixty concubines…."*

This is all making me feel seriously disadvantaged. Men can have all these wives and concubines but for a woman the rules are quite different.

Deuteronomy 22: 20 admonishes: *"If, though, this thing has proved to be the truth, evidence of virginity was not found in the girl, they must also bring the girl out to the entrance of her father's house, and the men of the city must pelt her with stones, and she must die...."*

What about a man's virginity – or otherwise? That never seems to count. Nowhere can I find even a vestige of concern for that. Always the woman is blamed and suffers.

And how about verse 23*: "In case a man is found lying down with a woman owned by an owner, both of them must then die together, the man lying down with the woman and the woman. So you must clear away what is bad out of Israel."*

Well at least that is a semblance of equality. Kill both equally! So a woman was owned by an owner – just a chattel, a possession, an object. Well, no thanks to the Bible-Word-of-God, but we have at least progressed on women's rights a bit since then.

St. Paul from 1 Corinthians 7:1 *"It is good for a man not to touch a woman."*

And 7:7-9: *"For I would that all men were as myself.... I say therefore to the unmarried and widows. It is good for them if they abide even as I. But if they cannot contain, let them marry: for it is better to marry than to burn."*

So that's how St. Paul sees our choice in life: Abstinence is best, marriage/sex-life is only for those who cannot 'contain' themselves and have to 'give in' to their natural nature! It makes such a monkey out of the real God, doesn't it? God – Creation – puts the most imperative drive in us, makes it as pleasurable as just about anything, and then men make up a religion in which, just as in the Garden of Eden, 'God' says, "You can play with any toy except the best one!" It's kind of psychotic to set one part against the other, one part teasing the other, testing the other, trying and judging the other. And that is supposed to be 'almighty god'!

HELP!

Here are some more of them, thanks to Barbara G Walker in *WEMS*:

Origen (Origenes Adamantius, Christian father, ca: 185-254 AD. An Egyptian who wrote in Greek, exerting a powerful influence on the early Greek church. Made a saint but declared a heretic three centuries later.): *"Matrimony is impure and unholy, a means to sexual passion."*

To St Jerome, the primary purpose of a man of God was to *'cut down with an axe of Virginity the wood of Marriage.'* And: *'Every man who loves his wife is guilty of adultery'!*

To St Ambrose, marriage was a crime against God, because it changed the state of virginity that God gave every man and woman at birth. Marriage was prostitution of the members of Christ, and *'married people ought to blush at the state in which they are living.'*

To Turtullian, marriage was a moral crime, *'more dreadful than any punishment or any death.'* It was *spurcitiae* – 'obscenity' or 'filth.'

To Tatian, marriage is corruption, *'a polluted and foul way of life.'* It seems he had such an effect on Syrian churches that only celibate men could become Christians!

According to Saturninus, God made only two kinds of people – good men and evil women!

St. Bernard said it was easier for a man to bring the dead back to life than to live with a woman without endangering his soul.

Well, there you have it. That is the old Christian view of marriage and women and that is from the time when Christianity was new and at its prime. So now all you married Christians know the church (secretly) disapproves of you. And all you good Christian women know your church (secretly) abhors you for not being a man.

The Bible-God-Chap Really Hates Women

Here are a few anti-women quotes:

St Paul in the first letter to Timothy decrees: "Let the women learn in silence with all subjection."

"But I suffer a woman not to teach, nor to usurp authority over a man, but to be in silence. For Adam was first formed then Eve." That Adam and Eve crap again!

"And Adam was not deceived, but the woman being deceived was in the transgression."

— 1Timothy 2:14-15

Let a woman learn in silence with full submissiveness? Where were you, Marquis de Sade. Just think what you missed – full church permission and encouragement!

St Paul reasons: *"For a man did not originally spring from woman, but woman was made out of man; and was not created for woman's sake, but woman for the sake of man."*

So again the misconstruing of the myth of Adam and Eve is used to hold woman in subjugation. Here is a bit more of Paul's 'wisdom': *"Wives submit to your husbands for the husband is the head of the wife as Christ is head of the Church. Now if the Church submits to Christ so should wives submit to their husbands in everything."*

And this:

"In like manner also, that women adorn themselves in modest apparel, with shamefacedness and sobriety; not with braided hair, or gold, or pearls, or costly array; but (which becometh women professing godliness) with good works."

— 1Timothy 2: 9-13

Well, what a charter of women's un-rights! And all based on a thorough misreading of the story of Adam and Eve.

Remember, God proved to be the liar and the Serpent the truth teller. Eve was therefore a great deal more prescient that Adam. And without Eve's courage to challenge 'God,' none of us would be here! So St. Paul is wrong on all counts. The very fabric of the Christian religion depends wholly on the misinterpretation of the myth of Adam and Eve. Here is Mary Daly from *Before God the Father* (Beacon Press, Boston 1973 p.69):

"Take the snake, the fruit tree, and the woman from the tableau, and we have no fall, no frowning Judge, no inferno, no everlasting punishment – hence no need of a Savior. Thus the bottom falls out of the whole Christian theology."

It seems the early Gnostic Christians – the real ones before the literalists got control, who were later branded as heretics – had a different idea. Here is Tertullian, appalled at the role of Gnostic women: "... *women of the heretics, how wanton they are! For they are bold enough to teach, to dispute, to enact exorcisms, to undertake cures, it may be even to baptize!*"

— Helen Ellerbe in *The Dark Side of Christianity*, (p.9)

And just generally appalled: *"The judgment upon your sex endures even today; and with it inevitably endures your position at the bar of justice. (Woman) you are the gateway to hell."*

— Tertullian in *De Cultu Feminarium*

What is it about saints?? Is part of being a saint that you hate woman, hate the feminine? Try this from St Jerome, Epistle 107: *"I am aware that some have laid it down that virgins of Christ must not bathe with eunuchs or married women, because the former still have minds of men and the latter present the ugly spectacle of swollen bellies. For my part I say that* ***mature girls should not bathe at all, because they ought to blush to see themselves naked."***

Hysterical! Where was he at? What on earth have all these 'saints' suffered so they hate and disparage their mothers, women and the feminine?

St. Gregory of Nazianzum was not too keen on women either: *"Women – a foe to friendship, an inescapable punishment, a necessary evil."*

"Among save beasts, none is found so harmful as woman."

St Paul again with another tenet clearly prohibits women from being ministers or otherwise speaking in church: *"Let your women keep silence in the churches: for it is not permitted unto them to speak"*

— 1Corinthians 14:34

Also from Corinthians 11:3 and 11:9:

"But I would have you know, that the head of every man is Christ; and the head of every woman is the man…."

"Neither was the man created for the woman, but the woman for the man."

St Clement of Alexandria (another 'saint') in the second century wrote: *"Every woman should be filled with shame by the thought that she is a woman."*

Isn't that just something! Let's see that again bold, uppercase and underlined so you don't miss it!

<u>EVERY WOMAN SHOULD BE FILLED WITH SHAME BY THE THOUGHT THAT SHE IS A WOMAN.</u>

Well you can't get more explicit than that. I trust all you Catholic Ladies like this sentiment and agree with it. And do you realize that up to the mid 16th century (see below), you were not even credited with having souls by your church. You were truly considered, and treated, like an inferior species.

THIS IS HISTORY, WOMEN, ***HIS***-STORY. ARE YOU HAPPY WITH IT? WHAT ABOUT ***HER***-STORY, WOMENS' STORY, YOUR STORY?

Turtullian – yes him again – endeavored to explain why women deserve their inferior status: *"And do you not know you are an Eve? The sentence of God on this sex of yours lives in this age: the guilt must necessarily live too."*

They all love to dump guilt on women, don't they. Was it that, like Augustine, he couldn't keep his pants on? He continues: *"You are the devil's gateway: you are the unsealer of that tree: you are the first deserter of the divine law: you are she who persuaded him whom the devil was not valiant enough to attack. You destroyed so easily God's image, man. On account of your desert – that is death – even the son of god had to die."*

So women get blamed for the death of Jesus! But Tertullian was mild compared to what was to come later. Boethius, a 6th century Christian 'philosopher' wrote in *The Consolation of Philosophy: "Woman is a temple built upon a sewer."*

And in Job 25:4 we read: *"How then can man be justified with God? Or how can he be clean that is born of woman?"*

All this is the literal 'word of god,' remember!

These guys must have had terrible problems with women's genitals and with sex and birthing. At the Council of Macon, apparently the bishops voted as to whether woman had souls at all. They decided not. Centuries later at the Council of Trent which took place from 1545 to 1563, I'm told it took one day for them to decide that animals don't have souls and 21 days and a close vote (majority of 3, I read) to decide that, perhaps after all, women do!

It seems there was no Christian marriage for centuries right up to and beyond the Council of Trent. This Council decreed that a person who even hinted that the state of matrimony might be more blessed than celibacy would be declared *anathema* – accursed and excommunicated!

Wife-beating was a normal Christian man's duty. The *Decretum* of 1140 said: "*It is right that he whom woman led into wrongdoing should have her under his direction so that he may not fail a second time though female levity.*"

Friar Cherubino's 15th century rules of marriage made the husband the wife's sole judge: "*Scold her sharply, bully and terrify her. And if this doesn't work take up a stick and beat her soundly, for it is better to punish the body and correct the soul than to damage the soul and spare the body… Then readily beat her, not in rage but out of charity and concern for her soul, so that the beating will redound to your merit.*"

— Abbreviated from Barbara G Walker, *WEMS*

This madness is our history, folks, and that bit is only 450 odd years ago. Here is the worst of all, from the infamous and appalling *Malleus Maleficorum* or *Witch's Hammer*: "*Because the female sex is more concerned with things of the flesh than men; because being formed from a man's rib, they are only imperfect animal and crooked whereas man belongs to a privileged sex from whose midst Christ emerged.*" Yet again it comes back to the Adam and Eve crap.

Bishop Epiphanus in the 4th century wrote (also quoted from p26 of above): "*God came down from heaven, the Word clothed himself in flesh from a holy virgin, not, assuredly, that the virgin should be adored, nor to make a goddess of her , nor that we should offer sacrifice in her name, nor that, now after so many generations, women should once again be appointed priests….(God) gave her no charge to minister baptism or bless disciples, nor did he bid her rule over the earth.*"

He was having a bit of difficulty making sure he got in all the things that shouldn't be done, wasn't he!

In the 5th century, the Catholic Church got really powerful. By 435 they had a law that threatened any heretic in the Roman Empire with death, (Hitler, Stalin where were you? You never managed anything like that!) and the only other legal religion was Judaism, though Jews were isolated and intermarriage carried the same penalty as adultery. Guess what that was – in this patriarchal society it was death for the woman, of course! What about the man? Not recorded.

Here are some anti-woman quotations from the Old Testament. Numbers 25 is interesting in its sheer violence: "*...Then the people started to have immoral relations with the daughters of Moab. And the women came calling the people to the sacrifices of their Gods... So Israel attached itself to Ba'al of Pe'or and the anger of Jehovah began to blaze against Israel. Hence Jehovah said to Moses, 'Take all the head ones of the people and expose them to Jehovah toward the sun that the burning anger of Jehovah may turn back from Israel. Each one of you KILL his men who have an attachment with the Ba'al of Pe'or.*

'But look, a man of the sons of Israel came bringing near to his brothers a Mid'ian-ite woman before Moses eyes... and the priest caught sight of it, he at once took a lance in his hand. Then he went after the man... and pierced both of them through, the man of Israel and the woman through her genital parts.... And those who died from the scourge amounted to ***twenty-four thousand.'"***

Well, I guess that put the kybosh on inter-marriage. Put the kybosh on a lot of lives, too.

Here is a funny one from Deuteronomy 25:11: "*In case men struggle together with one another and the wife of one has come near to deliver her husband out of the hand of the one striking him, and she has thrust out her hand and grabbed hold of him by his privates, you must then amputate her hand. Your eye must feel no sorrow."*

What? A wife tries to help her husband and has her hand cut off! Reading the Old Testament makes it so clear what an incredibly male-dominated, warlike, combative and violent time it was. And 'God' was the most warlike and violent of all. A very important question is - which comes first, 'God' or human society. Or perhaps better put - does 'God' create humans or do humans create 'God'? Clearly most of the time, it is we humans who create 'God' to suit our prevailing beliefs and what we see as our needs. So in a violent, warlike time when the greatest need is to be ready for combat – and the Middle East and Europe at the time had been in constant war for centuries, with empires coming and going and constant threats from neighbors – then a god of war was needed to keep the people in battle mode and the males in dominance. So that is what we got. *But let us stop pretending this has anything whatsoever to do with the real Creator-Creation.*

The Bible is the words of men and the 'gods' that the rulers required to bind their people together. By encouraging men to be warlike and dominant, to subdue not just anyone who doesn't agree with their dogma but the animals and plants and everything else around as well, the Bible has given carte blanche to the worst aspects of human nature and a 'god' who epitomizes them. So what about love? No person can make love and war at the same time. By frustrating the natural sexual instinct and making it wrong, and telling people God will be sending them to hell unless they crush their own natural instincts, the Bible version of religion has condemned us to an appalling travesty of the life we could have.

~ ~ ~

In the 15th and 16th centuries, the 'Reformation' – which I prefer to call the *Deformation* – the (even further) deforming of the human soul - spurned a load of virulent anti-woman preachers. Here is Martin Luther: *"Girls begin to talk and to stand on their feet sooner than boys because weeds always grow more quickly than good crops."*

What an incredibly convenient rationalization! Apparently the Lutherans debated whether women were really human beings at all! Martin Luther again, from *Table Talk: "Women … have but small and narrow chests, and broad hips, to the end that they should remain at home, keep house, and bear and bring up children."*

Sounds like a line from a Monty Python sketch. It would be funny except that it's real and countless women have suffered for such absurd beliefs.

John Knox, the Scottish Presbyterian leader also had little truck with women. From *The First Blast of the Trumpet Against the Monstrous Regiment of Women,* published 1558: *"Nature doeth paint them to be weak, frail, impatient, feeble and foolish; and experience hath declared them to be unconstant, variable, cruel, and lacking in the spirit of counsel."*

And this: *"To promote a woman to bear rule, superiority, dominion or empire, above any realm, nation, or city; contumely to God, a thing most contrarious to his revealed will and approved ordinance, and finally it is the subversion of good order, of all equity and justice."*

Well, I guess Queen Elizabeth 1 was not a Presbyterian. Nor Queen Elizabeth 2, or Margaret Thatcher or all those women MPs and woman leaders of one kind and another. I wonder if there are still any Presbyterians now – and are they all men? And how do they multiply and create more little Presbyterians?

And in the 18th century we get to this from Jonathan Edwards, a Calvinist New England theologian in the mid-1700s: *"(You are) a little, wretched, despicable creature: a worm, a mere nothing, and less than nothing; a vile insect that has risen up in contempt against the majesty of heaven and earth."*

~ ~ ~

Many years ago, I was researching in a library for something (ir)religious I could do in a comedy routine and to my delight I came across Edwards. The book said he was a 'major religious thinker of his day,' which made me cackle with delighted amazement at sheer human imbecility. Major religious thinker, indeed! That is an insult to the noble art of thinking. So let us look at some more of this 'major religious thinker's' astonishing 'religious thoughts' and enjoy a few good laughs. I suggest you think *Monty Python*, especially John Cleese in his Hitler / Basil Fawlty mode, all virulence and funny postures. Feel hate for everybody, screw up your face into a paroxysm of only-just-controlled violence, feel your body almost paralytic with stress, and then read this to your friends, spitting venom:

"The God that holds you over the pit of hell, much as one holds a spider or some loathsome insect over the fire, abhors you and is dreadfully provoked, his wrath towards you burns like fire; he looks upon you as worthy of nothing else but to be cast into the fire; he is of purer eyes than to bear to have you in his sight, you are ten thousand times so abominable in his eyes as the most hateful and venomous serpent is in ours."

Wow! You couldn't make it up so good. What was up with this guy? If he hated people so much, he must have deplored himself. Try this next one for the sheer appalling quality of fear and threat he is putting out:

"The bow of god's wrath is bent, and the arrow made ready on the string, and justice bends the arrow at your heart, and strains the bow, and it is nothing but the mere pleasure of God, and that of an angry God, without the promise or obligation at all, that keeps the arrow one moment from being made drunk with your blood."

Fabulous! Well fabulous to make comedy out of but not so good for the poor wretches who were in his congregation and had to listen to this soul-destroying shit Sunday after Sunday. Even worse for the unfortunates who actually took it to heart and believed it.

But there is more. Look at this next piece with sexual awareness. What sort of love and passion do you think this preacher might have enjoyed in his life? What sort of passion would lead a man to preach in this way? I know what I think but see what it says to you:

"The wrath of God is like the ***great waters*** *that are damned for the present.* ***They increase more and more****, and* ***rise higher and higher****, till an* ***outlet*** *is given: and the* ***longer the stream is stopped, the more rapid and mighty*** *is its course, when once* ***it is let loose****. It is true, that judgement against your evil work has not been executed hitherto; the* ***floods of God's vengeance*** *have been withheld, but your guilt in the meantime is* ***constantly increasing*** *and you are* ***every day treasuring up more*** *wrath; the* ***waters are continually rising and waxing more and more mighty*** *and there is nothing but the mere pleasure of God that holds the waters back that are* ***unwilling to be stopped and press hard*** *to go forward.*

"If God should only ***withdraw his hand from the floodgate****, it would* ***immediately fly open*** *and the* ***fiery floods of the fierceness and wrath*** *of God would* ***rush forth with inconceivable fury, and would come upon you with omnipotent power,*** *and if your strength were then thousand times greater than it is, yea, ten thousand times greater than the strength of the stoutest, sturdiest devil in hell, it would be nothing to withstand or endure it."*

OK, I cheated! I highlighted the best bits. This guy is monstrously frustrated. He is a sexual bomb waiting to go off, and he is obviously getting no release in the normal way, so his love implodes and becomes bottled venom and hate, and he seeks to control and dominate others so their love turns toxic, too. To see other people in a state of loving tenderness must have been quite unbearable to him.

And lastly, just to rub the point in, so to speak, how about this:

"There are the black clouds of God's wrath now hanging directly over your heads, ***full of the dreadful storm and big with thunder****, and were it not for the* ***restraining hand*** *of God, it would* ***burst forth*** *upon you. The sovereign pleasure of God, for the present, stays his rough wind; otherwise it would* ***come with fury*** *and your destruction would* ***come like a whirlwind*** *and you would be like the chaff on the summer threshing floor."*

— Jonathan Edwards, quoted from *Sinners in the Hands of an Angry God* (Boston, 1742)

Big … full of … restraining hand … come with fury … come like a whirlwind …

You can almost feel him orgasming in the preachers pulpit! And this man is a 'major religious thinker'?

Heyeokah says, "God save us from religion and its preachers."

'God' doesn't like the human body either. Funny sort of 'god' who hates his own creation, or did some other 'god' create the body? Here is St Paul:

Romans 8:5: *"For those who are in accord with the flesh set their minds on the things of the flesh, but those in accord with the spirit, on the things of the spirit."* So far so good.

8-6: *"For the minding of the flesh means death."* Funny, I always thought – in fact, I know – that minding the flesh, looking after the body, caring for it like it is my friend, keeps me fit, healthy and alive. *"… but the minding of the spirit means life and peace."* Yes, absolutely, but not if your body is falling apart through lack of care. Why is he so divided?

8-7: *"Because the minding of the flesh means enmity with God, for it is not under the subjection to the law of God, nor in fact can it be."* No it doesn't! Caring for your body is caring for your human temple, given by God-Creation for the purpose of this life. No body, no life! If 'God' is against the body, he is against life itself, and he is supposed to be the creator of all life! Well, if so – and this is the Bible so it 'must' be the 'word-of-god' – then god, by his own words, is seriously schizophrenic as one part of him is acting against the other!

8-9: *"However, you are in harmony not with the flesh but with the spirit, if God's spirit truly dwells within you."* Why can we not be in harmony with the flesh *and* the spirit? Seems much more whole and sensible to me.

8-13: *"For if you live in accord with the flesh you are sure to die, but if you put the practices of the body to death by the spirit, you will live."* This verse really shows the problem. They all seem to want to attack the body as if it is the enemy. If you kill the body, you will live – not in this realm you won't. Life after death – yes – but that comes to all of us in due time.

Turning to James 1:15, we read: *"Thus when lust hath conceived, it bringeth forth sin, when it is finished, bringeth forth death."*

Lust, you nincompoop, brings forth new life. No lust, no babies. Try and make love without it! Jolly difficult and requires a whole lot of fantasy - and that's a jolly big sin, remember. (See Chapter 2 if you forgot already!)

What a miserable outlook! I have demonstrated in earlier chapters the number of 'saints' who seem to have been unable to keep their pants on and blamed the women for their problems. It seems that as they were unable to control their own desires, they tried everything to control, restrict and limit the natural way of the body, thinking this was somehow 'godly.' They also lacked any sort of respect for the Earth. The Roman Empire built aqueducts, roads, houses with plumbing, washing facilities – we have all heard of Roman baths and there are relics in England – but once the Christians got to power, all that was neglected, and hygiene and 'things of the body' became considered contemptible and ungodly. In fact, it is really only in the last fifty to perhaps hundred years that decent bodily hygiene has come back into fashion in some Christian countries. Thanks to the leisure clubs, gyms, saunas, steam rooms and the ancient sweat lodge ceremony of the Native American people.

Here is an Augustinian priest and chaplain to the King of Poland (From *Delumeou* in *Sin and Fear*, quoted in *The Dark Side of Christian History*, p.160): *"Follow our Lord's example, and hate your body; if you love it, strive to lose it, says holy scripture, in order to save it; if you wish to make peace with it, always go armed,* ***always wage war against it; treat it like a slave****, or soon you yourself will be its unhappy slave."*

Happily I do *not* obey this injunction, not at all, not one little bit. I treat my body well, I feed it with love and care, endeavor to listen to it and respond to its needs, and I go regularly to the gym for healthy exercise and bathing. And I do my best to make loving, healthy, beautiful love when the moment and circumstances are right!

Here's Jesus as quoted in Luke 20:34-36:

"The children of this system of things marry and are given in marriage, but those who have been counted worthy of gaining that system of things and the resurrection from the dead neither marry nor are given in marriage. In fact neither can they die anymore for they are like the angels, and they are God's children by being children of the resurrection."

So to not marry, and by implication, to have no sex life, is taught as superior. Thus the anti-sexual teaching that sets people at war with themselves is authenticated and combined with a nice bit of convenient fantasy. Well, of course, if they are like angels, they will have no such problems because they will have no bodies! Angels do not have bodies! Haven't you noticed?

And in Matthew 19:12, Jesus goes even further:

"For there are some eunuchs, which were so born from their mother's womb: and there are some eunuchs, which were made eunuchs of men: and there be eunuchs, which have made themselves eunuchs for the kingdom of heaven's sake. He that is able to receive it, let him receive it."

So chopping off your genitals is the most holy thing you can do!

"Origen was highly praised for having castrated himself. Justin's 'Apologia' said proudly that Roman surgeons were besieged by faithful Christian men requesting the operation. Tertullian declared: 'The Kingdom of Heaven is thrown open to eunuchs.' Justin advised that Christian boys be emasculated before puberty, so their virtue was permanently protected.

"In St. Paul's day, Rome revered the self-castrated god Attis and Paul was an earnest admirer of Roman Culture, as shown by the fact that he Romanised his name, changing it from Saul to Paul."

There are numerous sayings of Paul which suggest that he himself was castrated and that he rated it as necessary for the highest spiritual achievement: *"I bear in my body the marks of the Lord Jesus."* (Galations 6.17)

"Moreover, those who belong to Christ Jesus impaled the flesh together with its passions and lusts." (Galations 5:24)

"I would they were even cut off which trouble you." (Galations 5:12

(Note: the words 'cut off' are a euphemism for castrated)

"The natural man receiveth not the things not of the Spirit of God; for they are foolishness unto him." (1Corinthians 2:14)

— From Barbara G.Walker, *The Woman's Encyclopedia of Myths and Secrets*, Harper SanFrancisco, pp.146 / 776.

So there you are. Now you know what to do, Christian guys, to prove yourselves as really good Christian men. Seriously though, this really takes the lid off Christian sexuality. No wonder I had such a terrible, confused puberty while trying to be a good Christian. I still had my sinful member daily or even by the minute, trying to lead me away from 'god' and into sin, sin and every day yet more sin! Remember that saying, a man thinks of sex every six or so many minutes? Oh sorry, not minutes, seconds!. No wonder Christianity has nothing to offer people at puberty other than 'don't' and 'shouldn't'. It is a religion that, albeit subtly and in some cases unconsciously, is really recommending castration as the most godly state of being!

Death as a threat to invoke fear; the body as the enemy; sex as a great evil; woman as an inferior being without a soul; castrated men the most holy? What was wrong with these people? Hadn't they noticed that without sex, none of us gets to be here. None, not one, no one gets to be born. And furthermore, you need a woman for it; men simply cannot do it on their own, however hard they try.

How about this from Colossians 3:5-6: *"Deaden therefore, your body members that are upon the earth as respects fornication, uncleanness, sexual appetite, hurtful desire, and covetousness, which is idolatory. On account of those things, the wrath of God is coming."*

Here it is again from another Bible translation: *"Put to death therefore what is earthy in you: immorality, passion, evil desire, and covetousness, which is idolatory. On account of these the wrath of God is coming."*

Let us look for a moment at how later followers of this body-hating belief system made out. Here is Ignatius Loyola, founder of the Jesuits: *"I am mere dung, I must ask our Lord that when I am dead my body be thrown on the dungheap to be devoured by the birds and dogs.... Must this not be my wish in punishment for my sins?"*

— *Delumeau* - Catholicism between Luther and Voltaire

And from John Calvin again:

"We are all made of mud, and this mud is not just on the hem of our gown, or on the sole of our boots or in our shoes. We are full of it, we are nothing but mud and filth both inside and outside."

— Delumeau – *Sin and fear*

(Both the above are from Helen Ellerbe, *The Dark Side of Christian History*.)

We can go back to Genesis 3:17-19 for the origin of these sentiments: *"Cursed is the ground on your account. In pain you will eat its produce all the days of your life. And thorns and thistles it will grow for you, and you must eat the vegetation of the field. In the sweat of your face you will eat bread until you return to the ground, for out of it you were taken. For dust you are and to dust you will return."*

This bible-god-chap punishes, curses, hates. He is nothing remotely like a God of Love. What went so wrong?

And now for something even worse: Holocaust – The Inquisition. We are accustomed to thinking of the terrible wipe-out of the Jews in the WWII as The Holocaust. But there is a much greater holocaust in our history and it still affects deeply the collective psyche of the descendents of Europeans. I refer to the centuries of burnings of so-called witches and heretics. It seems even Sir Thomas More, a man for perhaps not as many seasons as advertised, was not averse to burning heretics – which at its simplest means *he was happy to torture and murder those who didn't agree with him.*

From the time of the imposition of the Nicaean Creed by Constantine, so-called heresy – i.e., anyone who didn't agree with the orthodoxy of the day – was persecuted vehemently in order to keep the faith 'pure.' In other words, everyone had to agree to 'believe' what those in authority decreed was 'the truth' or else suffer torture and death. Super mega mind-control. Just as, once Stalin got hold of Russia, he systematically imposed his will upon the politics, politicians and people of the day by murdering or banishing to Siberia any who wouldn't submit to him, thus imposing a tyranny of belief in communism (his version of it), so the Christian Church systematically imposed its will upon the politics and people of its day and forced upon them a whole set of beliefs with the threat of torture and death.

George Orwell came up with the wonderful concept of the 'thought police' in his novel *1984*. But it was not in any way a new idea. They've been around for millennia as an arm of the Catholic Church.

It seems that, prior to Constantine, maybe as few as 2,000 people were tortured and murdered in the process of the battle by Rome against the early Christians up to the imposition of Christianity as the official religion of the empire. However, in the centuries following, as many as 25 million were murdered by the church as heretics. Add in the 12 million murdered in the conquest of the Americas plus the witch burnings and all that went on over approximately 14 centuries in order to impose this tyranny, and some say the total could well be in excess of 100 million. That is a lot of murder. Especially when done in the service of something people call 'god.'

It is important to realize that the length of time and the scope of this holocaust completely dwarfs those of either Hitler or Stalin. It went on in different parts of Europe from the 300s to as recently as about 1800s with the 'witches' of Salem in the US. It is estimated that between 9 and 12 million people were burned across the face of Europe as witches from the 12th century to the 17th century by the Unholy Inquisition.

Why am I going on about this? Because it is like a folk memory, deep in the psyche, a deep sense of fear and dread, a deep sense of disconnection from the Real Divine because so many terrible things were done in the name of God and Christ, so many centuries of living under the threat of torture and death if you didn't 'believe' and profess and act as you were ordered. To dare to find true spirituality and connection to the real Source, we must divorce ourselves from these religious imposters, and that means to confront centuries of fear and terror that have been embedded in the psyche of our ancestors and handed down to us subliminally. Once we truly reframe ourselves as part of The Whole, the Divine, the Creation, the All-That-Is, the Great Spirit, God (the real God that is ALL-THAT-IS and ALL-MIGHTY), we are no longer alone but part of All-One, and the whole separatist, reductionist, belief-without-knowledge Christian, Jewish, Islamic (and other) masculinist church edifices crumble to dust and we are set free.

To the Native American people, Holocaust means four to five hundred years of European conquest, murder, genocide, loss of homelands, loss of livelihood, loss of citizenship in their own country, prohibition of their spiritual ways, loss of their whole way of life. Literalist Christian religion was very helpful in that it placed these people as 'lost souls' in need of 'saving.' Therefore 'god' would approve all the murder and genocide, and consider that every soul 'brought to Jesus' was worth all the bloodshed, lies and deceit. Weird sort of 'god.' And it's still going on now, too.

Holocaust to the Incas meant the arrival of Pizarro and his band of Spanish thugs. To the Aztecs, it meant the arrival of Cortez and his murderous army.

The Unholy Inquisition

In some parts of what the Roman Catholic Church considered to be its empire or fiefdom, it seems that around the later 1200s, they felt they were losing control. Pope Gregory IX appointed the Dominicans as inquisitors and ordered them to eradicate heresy everywhere. It is interesting to note that one root of the word 'heresy' is Hera, the wife of Zeus. Zeus was the Greek god of war - a role model for Jehovah – but his wife, Hera, had followers too who had different ideas. And they were called Heretics!

In and around 1308 AD in Southern France, the Cathars had different ideas, too, about God and worship and it seems the Catholic Church was seriously frightened it was *losing control.* And losing control is not what the Church was about, so something had to be done. And it was. The Dominicans moved in and, after much inquisiting, torture, prison and burning at the stake, the Cathars were completely wiped out. Here is some background info:

Cathars and Catharism in the Languedoc (from www. languedoc-france.info):

"The Cathars were a religious group who appeared in Europe in the eleventh century, their origins something of a mystery. Records from the Roman Church mention them under various names and in various places, occasionally throwing light on basic beliefs. The Roman Church debated with itself whether they were Christian heretics or whether they were not Christians at all. In the Languedoc, famous at the time for its high culture, tolerance and liberalism, Catharism took root and gained more and more adherents during the twelfth century. By the early thirteenth century, it was probably the majority religion in the area, supported by the nobility as well as the common people. This was too much for the Roman Church, some of whose own priests had become Cathars. Worst of all, Cathars of the Languedoc refused to pay their tithes.

"The Pope, Innocent III, called a formal crusade, appointing a series of leaders to head his (un)holy army. There followed over forty years of war against the indigenous population. In 1233 the next pope, Gregory IX, charged the Dominican

Inquisition with the final solution: the absolute extirpation of the Cathars. Soon the Franciscans would join in, too, but it is St. Dominic and his followers who have left the legacy of hatred that endures into the third millennium. During this period, some 500,000 Languedoc men women and children were massacred; the Counts of Toulouse and their vassels were dispossessed and humiliated, and their lands annexed to France. Educated and tolerant Languedoc rulers were replaced by relative barbarians; the Dominican Order was founded and the Inquisition was established to wipe out the last vestiges of resistance; persecutions of Languedoc Jews and other minorities were initiated; the high culture of the Troubadours was lost; lay learning was discouraged; tithes were enforced; the Languedoc started its economic decline, and the language of the area, Occitan, started its descent from one of the foremost languages in Europe to a regional dialect.

"At the end of the extirpation of the Cathars, the Church had convincing proof that a sustained campaign of genocide can work. It also had the precedent of an internal Crusade within Christendom, and the machinery of the first modern police state. This crusade was one of the greatest disasters ever to befall Europe. Catharism is often said to have been completely eradicated by the end of the fourteenth century. Yet there are more than a few vestiges even today, apart from the enduring memory of their martyrdom and the ruins of the famous Cathar castles. There are even Cathars alive today, or at least people claiming to be modern Cathars."

It became recognized that joining the Inquisition could be a good career move for a priest and for a certain Father Jacques Fournier, that certainly turned out to be true. He was the primary inquisitor in the Cathar village of Montaillou and after 'successfully' trying 98 cases of 'heresy,' he became a cardinal and eventually Pope Benedict XII. His approach to those who didn't see it his way was 'convert or die.' This demand was backed up by monstrous instruments of torture and the ultimate of burning at the stake. The people mostly accused of witchcraft were the healers who were mainly women and who used herbs and folk remedies of their time. These were all deemed satanic and a reason for accusation of all sorts of things.

"The Inquisition worked by ignoring all rules of natural justice. Guilt was assumed from the start. The accused had no right to see the evidence against them, or their accusers. They were not even told what the charges were against them. They had no right to legal counsel, and if exceptionally they were allowed a legal representative then the representative risked being arrested for heresy as well.

"People were charged on the say-so of hostile neighbors, known enemies and professional informers who were paid on commission. False accusations, if exposed, were excused if they were the result of 'zeal for the Faith.' Guilty verdicts were assured, especially since, in addition to their punishment, half of a guilty person's property was seized by the Church. (The Dominicans soon hit on the idea of digging up and trying dead people, so that they could retrospectively seize their property).

"Techniques of obtaining confessions included threats of procedures against other family members, promises of leniency in exchange for a confession, trick questions, sleep deprivation, indefinite imprisonment in a cold dark cell on a diet of bread and water, and, of course, a wide range of even more ghastly techniques. Torture was a favorite method of extracting confessions for offences both real and fabricated. Its use was explicitly sanctioned by Pope Innocent (Guilty) IV in 1252 in his bull *ad extirpanda*. Inquisitors and their assistants were permitted to absolve one another for applying torture. Instruments of torture, like crusaders' weapons, were routinely blessed with holy water.

"Torture was applied liberally to obtain whatever confessions were required, and sometimes just to punish people that the Church authorities did not like. Together, these techniques were responsible for the first police state in Europe, where the only thoughts and actions permitted were those approved of by the Roman Church, where no one could be trusted, and where duty to the totalitarian authority took precedence over all other duties, whether those duties were to one's chosen sovereign, family, friends, beliefs, conscience, or even to the truth."

Catholics, this is the history of your religion. Is this the doings of a 'God' and a church you really want to worship? Catholic ladies – this is the time before your church even granted you a soul, so in those days, you were a non-person!

The atmosphere that the Inquisition produced is similar that achieved by Stalin in his heyday, so well portrayed by George Orwell in *1984*, and also of Hitler in the 1930s as he built up Nazism and the Hitler youth. In all these cases, such fear was produced that all trust broke down. Neighbors were incriminating neighbors, members of the same family were incriminating each other, and even children were denouncing their own parents. What an incredible decimation of a society. Such incredible wickedness in the name of 'God.'

The Inquisition went on to Spain – Iberia as it was then called. Up to this time, Christians, Moslems and Jews had lived side-by-side in a state of mutual tolerance and respect known as 'convivensia.' This was too much for the Catholic Church and Pope Sixtus IV sent the Inquisition to create years of horror and decimate that society. There was a pogrom against the Jews and again the demand to convert or die.

Next on the list was Venice, which at that time was a Republic in its own right and which did not wish to be dominated by Rome. This was the time when Martin Luther and the Protestants were gaining power in northern Europe and the Catholic Church was again terrified of *losing control!* A certain Bishop Caraffa was dispatched, along with the usual small army of church mercenaries, to stamp out heresy. Apparently he was very upset by the University of Padua, which was full of free-thinkers so he set out to change that. He was a true zealot and reputedly said, "Even if my own father were a heretic, I would gather the wood to burn him."

Well, you can't get more extreme than that. Well, not if you're a true zealot – which in today's language means bigot.

When he became Pope Paul IV – yes for him, too, it was a good career move – he set about stamping out the Jews. He issued a Papal Bull that overturned hundreds of years of tolerance and, by 1557, Jews were forbidden to own any books except the Bible. So 200 years after being driven out of Spain, and welcomed into multi-cultural Venice, the Jews found themselves being driven out again.

Mind you, all was not milk and honey for Pope Paul IV. It seems that when he died in 1559, Rome celebrated his death with considerable joy and partying as he was a truly hated man. Among the many acts he did to prevent human advancement, was to create a long list of books that he deemed prohibited. *And this list of forbidden books was not abolished by the Catholic Church until 1966!*

In the late 1700s, Napoleon was a serious enemy of the Inquisition (no wonder I like Napoleon Brandy!) and worked tirelessly to keep them out of his territory. When he was deposed. they got back in to create more havoc and misery. In 1796. Spain was again terrorized by them. In 1858, they were in full swing in the papal states of Italy … and continued for four more decades. They created untold misery for almost 600 years across the face of Europe, just to keep the power of the Catholic Church over the people. All of us who know anything about spiritual truth know that witchcraft, as represented by them, is a totally false idea. The people they deemed witches were, in the main, healers, folk doctors and herbalists. Perhaps one day, the real meaning of witch – 'wise woman' – will be restored to popular culture.

Here is a little about the doings of the Inquisition in England from Barbara G. Walker in *WEMS*:

"From ruthlessly organized persecutions on the continent, witch-hunts in England became largely cases of village feuds and petty spite. If crops failed, horses ran away, cattle sickened, wagons broke, women miscarried, or butter wouldn't come in the churn, a witch was always found to blame. Marion Cumlaquay of Orkney was burned in 1643 for turning herself three times widdershins to make her neighbor's barley crop rot. A tailor's wife was executed for quarrelling with her neighbor, who afterward saw a snake on his property, and his children fell sick. One witch was condemned for arguing with a drunkard in an alehouse. After drinking himself into paroxysms of vomiting, he accused her of bewitching him, and he was believed.

"A woman was convicted of witchcraft for having caused a neighbor's lameness … by pulling off her stockings. Another was executed for having admired a neighbor's baby which afterward fell out of its cradle and died. Two Glasgow witches were hanged for treating a sick child, even though the treatment succeeded and the child was cured. Joan Cason of Kent went to the gallows in 1586 for having dry thatch on her roof."

Utter madness, a whole culture gone psychopathic. It must have been a truly appalling time to live. The Church put back medical knowledge by an incalculable amount and brought untold misery, sickness and hardship by murdering the medical profession of the time. Imagine the Church of England branding the

National Health Service as evil and killing off all the doctors and nurses by public burning! Mind you, right now another fundamentalist power is trying to take away our freedom to treat ourselves with vitamins and herbs – the 'Church of Big Pharma.' Big powerful pharmaceutical companies are vying for legislation to prevent us buying health supplements and keeping ourselves well. It seems they'd benefit so much more if we were all sick and had to be on medication. I read an incredible statistic recently – the average American takes one medication a day and no less than 17% are on 3 medications per day.

It seems probable that the Inquisition was directly responsible for between nine and twelve million people who were tortured, burned, and/or imprisoned in appalling circumstances. God knows how many had their lives ruined and how many cultures suffered appalling decimation. A friend researched for me and found records dating back to 1234 when 8,000 'Stedingers' (not sure who they were) were burned. Then 1239, 180 were burned for witchcraft at Montwinmer in France, and in 1275, Angela de la Barthe was burned at Toulouse.

The last in Europe would seem to be 100 people in Haeck, Germany between 1772 and 1779, 2 in Poland in 1793, several in South America in the 1800s, 1 in Illinois in 1870 and 5 in Mexico in 1877. In the last century, apparently one person was shot by a policeman in Uttenheim, Germany in 1925 on suspicion of being a werewolf, and one killed for 'sorcery' in France as recently as 1977! In Africa, hundreds are killed on suspicion of witchcraft – right up to August 2000 – and who knows just how much of this still goes on.

In response to church inquisitors demanding he recant his knowledge that the Earth revolves around the Sun, under threat of good Christian torture and death of course, Galileo Galilei said: *"I do not feel obliged to believe that the same God who has endowed us with sense, reason, and intellect has intended us to forgo their use."*

The Inquisition is a terrible blot on our history. Hitler and Stalin, appalling as they were, were short term blips by comparison, though at least they didn't pretend to be doing it for 'god.' Let us try to see nothing like it ever happens again.

Heyeokah Guru says: *God save us from religion!*

I have criticized St Paul quite a bit in this chapter so here is one piece he got right:

"But if there be no resurrection of the dead, then is Christ not risen: And if Christ be not risen, then our preaching is in vain, and your faith is also vain. Yea, and we are found false witnesses of God, because we have testified of God that he raised up Christ whom he raised not up, if so be that the dead rise not.'

— Corinthians 15:13-16

YES, YES, YES, YES, YES, YES, YES AND YES AGAIN!

Chapter 7

Nothing Is Perfect Except Everything

Christianity has embraced the idea of God as 'perfect' and human beings as a bunch of miserable sinners and bad people. This necessitates the invention of a counter force to explain all the things that go wrong so 'god' can stay pure and unsullied, and be seen to do only the good things of creation. So they had to invent 'The Devil' to take responsibility for everything they didn't like and everything that went wrong.

But if God is already perfect, why on earth bother with all this creation, with this planet, with the galaxy, with the whole Universe? The Creator must have some reason, some purpose however mysterious, to Create Itself into the Creation.

Furthermore, how could a 'perfect' God keep screwing up so badly that this other devil-chap keeps getting in and making a mockery of his plans? If the god-chap was at all perfect, or even competent, he would have sussed out the devil-chap long ago and got him sorted!

Surely the reason for God, The Source, to create Itself into all this Life, The Universe and Everything is to gain experience, to grow, to develop, to evolve. *Life is the manifested evidence of the Source's Desire for Evolution* – the same desires that are in us, though on a giant scale. Of course, we live within God, The Source,

Infinite Creator, so how can we not feel the same feelings as God, and God the same feelings as us, albeit at a vastly different level of existence and very different level of consciousness?

The notion of perfection within earthly existence is a silly, misguided myth created by cultures that have lost their connection with the natural roots of existence. Just look at nature. The whole of nature is perfect in an overall sense but try to find a flower without a blemish, an animal without a mark of some kind, a human without a problem, a tree without a dead branch? Everything has its imperfection – that's nature. Perfection / imperfection live together in balance. Look at the lupin flower. You will never find a perfectly flowering lupin. When it is fully bloomed at the bottom, some of the top is dead, and when it is flowering perfectly at the top, the bottom hasn't yet budded!

The religious idea that humanity is separate from God has caused immeasurable misery, confusion and loss of inner authority. Together with the absurd travesties of original sin and the trashing of the proper meaning and teaching of the story of Adam and Eve, this has left us floundering in a sea of cock-eyed back-to-front life-myths that leave us disenfranchised from our own selves and from the very Nature that gave rise to us in the first place.

Note this: The Universe lives in a state of dynamic disequilibrium. DIS-equilibrium. Slight, subtle, but nevertheless there. The Taoists have a saying: "The yin is never completely yin and the yang is never completely yang."

Phi is the Golden Mean or Fibonacci Ratio after the 16th century mathematician Leonardo de Pisa, calculated by adding the last number to the present number to get the next one: i.e., 1, 1, 2, 3, 5, 8, 13, 21, 34, 55, etc. When you boil that down to a ratio – and it is found throughout nature – it is a ratio that never resolves. 1.618……….. forever

Look at pi, the ratio of the diameter of a circle to the circumference. 3.142….. That, too, never resolves.

Just suppose these numbers did resolve and the yin did become totally yin and the yang totally yang, what then?

Well, everything would reach equilibrium. How wonderful you might think. Now we can all stop worrying and have a nice cup of tea. Or something stronger, perhaps. Ahh, but that in itself will recreate disequilibrium!

No, the point is that everything would stop moving and changing. Stop moving, stop changing, become static, the same, unchanging, no growth, no energy, no development, no future, no progression. And that means no life.

The Universe must exist in dis-equilibrium, in perfect imperfection, in order to exist as an ongoing creation. What is actually so amazing is that the illusion of existence we experience is so consistent! That the necessary state of dis-equilibrium is so subtle as to be virtually unapparent.

Now back to the Bible-god-chap. What would a screw-up of a god-chap naturally demand to keep your allegiance, no matter what messes he makes and how cleverly the devil-chap pisses on his plans? What else but …

YOUR BLIND, UNTHINKING FAITH!

Well, he would, wouldn't he?

Tertullian says: *"We want no curious disputation after possessing Christ Jesus, no inquisition after enjoying the gospel! With our faith, we desire no further belief.*

"This rule … was taught by Christ, and raises amongst ourselves no other questions than those which heresies introduce, and which make men heretics."

And he adds: *"Credo quia incredibilis est,"* or in English: *"I believe because it is unbelievable."*

And this: "*... I maintain that the Son of God was born; why am I not ashamed of maintaining such a thing? Why! But because it is itself a shameful thing. I maintain that the son of God died: well that is wholly credible because it is monstrously absurd. I maintain that after having been buried, he rose again: and that I take to be absolutely true, because it was manifestly impossible!*"

— Quoted by Rudolf Steiner in *Christianity as Mystical Fact* (Anthroposophic Press, 1972)

Well, that is what Tertullian said. Make of it what you will. I'd recommend him a series of appointments with a good psychotherapist.

St. Augustine, quoted from Archarya S (p.24) said: *"I should not believe in the truth of the Gospels unless the authority of the Catholic Church forced me to do so."*

Quite a statement! She says he had already accepted 'as historic truth the fabulous founding of Rome by Romulus and Remus, their virgin-birth by the god Mars, and their nursing by the she-wolf...'

The 2nd century Epicurian philosopher Celsus, who in common with most of the Grecians, looked upon Christianity as a: "*blind faith that shunned the light of reason,*" said of the Christians: *"They are forever repeating: 'Do not examine. Only believe, and thy faith will make thee blessed. Wisdom is a bad thing in life; foolishness is to be preferred.'"*

In the 4th century, Bishop Irenaeus of Lyons said:

"It is incumbent to obey the priests who are in the church (well, that is the whole point, isn't it – church control of everything including thinking) ... *those who possess the succession from the apostles;*

those who, together with the succession of the episcopate, have received the certain gift of truth."

Truth? Truth based on fiction, deceit, lies, fabrications and fantasies and aimed at mass brainwashing. Remarkably successful it was too, for an incredibly long time, but enough. It's time for some truth from the place of investigation, from the place of freedom to seek, sort, sift, weigh up and evaluate. Truth from the place of real wisdom.

For hundreds of years, just questioning the 'word-of-god' was in itself considered heresy. As with Stalinist communism, a person had no right to question the orthodoxy, no right to his or her own opinion, at least not to discuss it with others, let alone express it publicly. The potential price for doing so was some horrible death, so it's not surprising that the populace was kept under subjection. We know this as 'totalitarianism' but in those days it was 'correct religious belief,' and all 'good people' adhered strictly to it. Such a policy brings about a homogenous society and makes it easy to keep order with minimal policing. It's particularly effective when you can get the orthodoxy so strong and the fear element so great that neighbors will rat on neighbors, bosses on their employees, staff on their employers, children on parents, brothers on sisters. This creates a truly terrible society to live in but the most controllable one from the point of view of the dominators. It kills the human spirit, crushes the soul, stifles the emotions and nullifies the ability to think. Just what all good psychopaths want.

When the Church succeeded in taking over in Europe by circa 500 AD, instead of an age of love and light as 'Gentle Jesus' might have been expected to bring, we got the Dark Ages, centuries of ignorance, of a darkness in education (read only the Bible please, and burn all other books), science (no knowledge unless it is in the Bible, please), history (only what is written in the Bible), medicine (same), art (only 'approved' art on approved religious themes, thank you). A thousand years later, Galileo had to recant his truth to save being butchered by those determined to maintain ignorance.

This was the time that orthodox Christians suppressed as much knowledge as they could by burning books. (I can already hear cries for this one to be burned! Those who seek to dominate always hate truth.) In A.D. 391 the Roman-appointed Bishop Theophilus led a mob into the Serapeum quarter of Alexandria and burned the Alexandrian library. The librarian was a brilliant and beautiful woman named Hypatia, so the mob stripped her and carved the flesh off her bones while she was still alive. All in the name of God, of course. (In *Christianity: An Ancient Egyptian Religion*, author Ahmed Osman says the library was burned to destroy all records of the actual Egyptian roots of Christianity.) They closed the then equivalent of universities and restricted education to priests and those in the approved (i.e., controllable) occupations.

In 398 at the 4th Council of Carthage, bishops and presumably all clergy were forbidden to read any books not written by Christians!

Oh the glories of ignorance. So little to think about, so little to concern oneself with, so few problems to sort out, no creativity whatsoever to waste time on ….

This stupendous stupidity still goes on and is present amongst us in the 21st century. I recently saw it on TV in the debate of the imbeciles versus the nincompoops!

I listened to this most extraordinary debate that is going on in the USA between those in favor of Darwin and his scientific ideas of evolution and those who want to bring back the godchap and say that the Universe was 'Intelligently Designed' by this chap in 4004 BC, an extraordinary contradiction in itself!

Well, if I say I'm 'not impressed,' will you fill in the unprintable blanks for me? I watched this BBC *Horizon* TV program and had to get a bottle of best Napoleon brandy to stop myself throwing things at the screen and making a nasty mess. I'm not sure how the neighbors got on with my virulent guffaws, but then I live with tolerant friends.

First of all, is there any sensible person anywhere out there who thinks the universe is created *unintelligently?* That the incredibly way it all works is some sort of cosmic accident? Or that it 'just happened'? Or that it is a purposeless, Matrix-like computer game some crazy cosmic unidentified lunatic is playing at our expense? If you do think that, Heyeokah Guru recommends you look in a mirror to see a nincompoop.

A small study of sub-atomic quantum physics will reveal to you an amazing universe, just as will a study of the heavens and the galaxies and the amazing complexity of the stars and planets out there. It all hangs together and has for an inconceivably long time, and here we are on one itsy-bitsy little planet, journeying around a small star on an outer wing of a minor galaxy, one of several hundred billion galaxies. Some imbecile inhabitants of this little planet seem to think we are the only intelligent species in the whole of Creation – a most supremely idiotic idea in itself!

Now, a little history. Darwin's theory of evolution (*Origin of Species,* 1859) shattered the Bible beliefs of that time and so was seen as questioning the very existence of the god-chap. In the 19th century, religion was weaker than it used to be, so they couldn't burn Darwin as a heretic or even burn all his books, and they rather lost out as Darwin's ideas gradually became the orthodoxy in schools. Now we are witnessing a backlash as the Bible-people want to restore their chap to his former dominance and reduce children to a state of malleable ignorance. As per this from James Dobson in *Children at Risk: The Battle for the*

Hearts and Minds of our Kids (World Publishing, 1990, p.35): *"Children are the prize in the second great civil war. Those who control what young people are taught and what they experience – what they see, hear, think, and believe – will determine the future course for the nation."*

Translation: Whoever can brainwash our kids controls the future.

No wonder there is such a row going on about how Creation is taught in schools. They think kids are stupid enough to believe what they are told in school? May our kids be bright enough to foil any such nonsense!

According to the TV program, the religionists came up with a thing called a 'flagellum' that they said could not be reduced to its component parts. This was supposed to 'prove' that the god-chap had spontaneously created it. hence 'proving,' with monumental stupidity, the theory of 'Intelligent Design' and making Darwin no longer correct so he could be banished out of schools and replaced by Bible dogma. Well, hard as they tried, inevitably someone came up with the answer they didn't want and showed that the jolly flagellum is just like everything else and is developed out of smaller bits that have been around before.

The whole debate is so ridiculous that I sat there wondering what small percentage of humans are actually intelligent. I felt I was watching imbeciles debating nincompoops. Rather than intelligent design of the cosmos, how about some intelligent design – or just simple intelligence – amongst humans?

How can the Universe not be intelligently designed when it is so intelligent? The innate intelligence that is in the Universe is itself the intelligence of God, of Creation. When scientists and biologists study the workings of the Universe, they are studying the workings of God. When quantum physicists study the particles and waves that make up the fabric of the manifest

Universe, they are studying the inner fabric of God; when astrophysicists study the workings of the stars and galaxies, they are studying the outer fabric of God. When psychologists study the inner workings of a human being, they are studying the workings of God embodied into an individual self-reflective being who is not yet fully conscious of who s/he is. There is no problem until you try to separate God and the Universe, as if the Universe is something separate that the god-chap did or didn't create.

Darwin may well be wrong, too, as it seems human bones have been discovered alongside dinosaur bones, so the human race may well be far older than generally thought. (See the quote from Professor Dan Smail in Chapter 1.) And we may even be a genetically created species by the 'sky-gods' coming down and mating with the 'daughters of the earth.' I do not pretend to know, but one thing is sure: Current consensus thinking is bunk! We have an enormous amount to discover about our real history, and only a total brainwashed imbecile idiot could think some god-chap created it all in seven days in 4004 BC!

We have seen just how much of religious 'orthodoxy' is pure made up manipulation for political ends. So let us come to the real nature of god, and to do this we return to the very beginning where in Genesis, I commented in Chapter 1 on the change of voice between the two creation stories that the Bible begins with. In the first story-myth, God creates everything in the order it obviously was created in, and man is born of woman. In the second story, a quite different 'god-chap' appears who interacts with humans, spends most of his time angry, is amazingly vengeful and belligerent, kills just for the hell of it, condemns anyone he doesn't like to eternal torment, and shows himself to be a thoroughly nasty piece of work. Most of the Bible seems to be about this latter monster and misses spirituality, love, care, respect and even bodily hygiene. How on earth have so many people believed this crap for so long? And isn't it totally amazing that some still do, in this the 21st century?

It doesn't have to be that way. Here is a quote from that wonderful book by Thomas Moore, *Care of the Soul* (Piatkus Books, 1992, p.229):

"The history of our century has shown the proclivity of neurotic spirituality toward psychosis and violence. Spirituality is powerful and therefore has the potential force for evil, as well as for good. The soul needs spirit, but our spirituality also needs soul – deep intelligence, a sensitivity to the symbolic and metaphoric life, genuine community, and attachments to the world.

"We have no idea yet of the positive contribution that could be made to us individually and socially by a more soulful religion and theology. Our culture is in need of theological reflection that does not advocate a particular tradition, but tends the soul's need for spiritual direction. In order to accomplish this goal, we must gradually bring soul back to religion, following Jung, who wrote in a letter of 1910 to Freud, 'What infinite rapture and wantonness lie dormant in our religion. We must bring to fruition its hymn of love.'"

Well, yes, great, such possibility … but not if we collectively continue to worship (by his own words as shown in Chapter 3) a violent, angry, vicious, intolerant, devious, bigoted, racist, psychopathic, paranoid, schizophrenic, murderous, homophobic, misogynistic domineering egotist who favors rape of young girls and slavery – and call him 'god.' That, at the very least, is surely a massive insult to Infinite Creator/Creation. It also says an uncomfortable lot about the state of human intelligence.

This is the 21st century and people are still worshipping this … thing. (I don't know what to call it that is printable.)

We become what we worship. If we worship a deity of Love, Compassion and Cooperation, we will become that. If we worship the 'god' described above, we will become that. Many have. Many still do. Great Pity.

LOOK AROUND YOU! IT'S TIME TO WAKE UP.

Chapter 8

The Imbalanced Trinity

'Polarity is the loom on which reality is strung.'

— Mayan Oracle

Most spiritual teachings express the godhead as a trinity. This trinity consists of:

1. All-That-Is
2. The Feminine
3. The Masculine

Or as expressed in the Far East:

1. All
2. Yin
3. Yang

In essence, all ancient trinities show the Ultimate Creator as All-Potential that became All Manifestation in its two polarities, Feminine and Masculine.

Native American cosmology expresses it as:

1. Great Spirit / Great Mystery (unknowable, unlimited)
2. Great Grandmother Wakan (all that is feminine)
3. Great Grandfather Ssquan (all that is masculine)

Our Pagan ancestors likewise saw Creation as a trinity of balance. However, when we get to our world today, an extraordinary difference has occurred. The commonly accepted Christian trinity is:

1. God the Father (masculine)
2. God the Son (masculine)
3. God the Holy Ghost (non-gender)

WHATEVER HAPPENED TO THE FEMININE?

We all know that human creation takes one man and one woman, one masculine energy and one feminine energy. Not even the most dedicated same-sex couples have ever managed to create offspring. So how come we expect the gods to do it? It is completely against everything that we know and everything that is natural!

Now when a culture holds as sacred a trinity that is all masculine, it stands to reason that the feminine energy has been seriously demoted, if not virtually deleted, from any place of power.

So just look at what we have done to the primal feminine energy – EVE, Our Mother, the Earth. Is it any wonder that, as a culture, we show her no respect, we pollute her, desecrate her, use up her resources carelessly, throw our trash on her, rape her …. It's as if the son has usurped the mother in the family trinity and so the mother is now pushed aside, shat on, desecrated and reduced to mere servant or even slave.

It is time for a radical *solution* and there is one:

It is time for our religions to face this dreadful error and correct this imbalance by correcting their mistake and bringing the feminine back into the trinity:

God the Father
God the Mother
God the Holy Ghost

Every Sunday, thousands of people go to churches and worship 100% imbalance. What a monumental difference it would make if this were to change. Our Mother is suffering from our lack of love for her, from our collective lack of care for her. Our religious leaders focus on the idea of 'saving souls' but if they do not help in the saving of our mother, the Earth, they will have no souls to 'save.' The most important issue right now is ecology of the Earth. The other most important issue is ecology of the human being which also requires a balance of masculine and feminine.

Here is different concept of Trinity – the Hindu concept: Brahman (the 'Creator' God) *is* his Creation. The cosmos is not so much a creation, but more an emanation from Brahma, the Ultimate Creator.

All humans, animals, gods, and even objects, are One-Divine-Being. The soul of each person is thus Brahman, the entirety of creation, and every animal or stone or star is an aspect of Brahman. This may be a difficult concept to comprehend if you are accustomed to thinking of God as a separate chap in a separate place – the 'Santa Claus-for-grownups' – for how can the "small" soul of each person or even a stone be one with the "large" god of the cosmos? But it is the comprehension of this very idea that is a central goal of human life and in the resolution of the human problem in Hinduism and also in the ancient spiritual paths of humans of planet Earth. The multiplicity that hides the cosmos' unity, the Hindus call Maya; that is the reality humans perceive with their senses everyday. The overcoming of Maya to perceive True Reality (Brahman) constitutes 'The Task' in Hinduism. You and God are one.

So, for Hinduism, there may be millions of gods! However, these gods are not God-God, they cannot create stars, or planets, or plants or animals – or humans. "Brahman" is The Absolute, the Real God.

Though believed wrongly by many to be a polytheistic religion, the basis of Hinduism is the belief in the unity of everything. This totality is called Brahman, the Absolute, the Supreme Being, the Ultimate Reality, the Divine. The purpose of life is to realize that we are part of God. For most Hindus, this God is not a person but a force, an energy, a principle.

All the so-called pantheistic religions I have studied have, under the Pantheon, this same concept of Oneness, Unity, Absolute, Single Beingness. This Unity we can call Creator *is the Creation*. In the ancient shamanistic spiritual ways of the hunter-gatherers, the cosmos is seen as a Unity and its expression is nature. This Native American medicine wheel, known as the Earth Count, tells of this understanding of Creation poetically:

In the beginning was the Great Round, the Zero, the No-Thing which is the potential of All Things, the Womb of all Life that births All Existence. All the Children of Creation are designed in the Zero and from the Zero come forth into manifestation.

The Zero is the Marriage of All-That-Is-Feminine – Great Grandmother Wakan – and All-That-Is-Masculine – Great Grandfather Ssquan, the Lightning Bolt who potentizes the zero of potential into manifestation.

Creation, for us, began when Great Grandmother Wakan and Great Grandfather Ssquan made Love and gave birth to their first born, Grandfather Sun.

Grandfather Sun is given the number One. He rises in the East, so we place him on the Medicine Wheel in the Easterly Direction.

Great Grandfather and Great Grandmother made love a second time and gave birth to Grandmother Earth. Grandmother is given the number Two, and we place her opposite the Sun on the West of the Wheel.

Then Grandfather Sun and Grandmother Earth made love and they gave birth to their first born, the Kingdom of Plants. The plants thrive in the summer and they depend on water so we place them in the South direction of the Wheel. Their number is Three which is the sum of One and Two.

Grandmother and Grandfather made love again and gave birth to their second born, the Kingdom of Animals. The animals breathe the air and we place them on the North of the wheel. Their number is Four which is the sum of One and Two plus One.

Grandmother and Grandfather made love a third time and gave birth to their third born, the Kingdom of Humans. The place of the Humans is in the Center of the Wheel but towards the South because Humans are as yet children of the Cosmos. We are the one kingdom that is still incomplete and we are still learning who we are. Our number is Five.

Number six is our ancestors and our history. Six is the number of all directions: East, West, South, North, Above and Below. Six is placed in the Southeast direction between fire and water.

Seven is the number of the six directions plus the power of Light (One). It is the 'Dream' of Creation. In the energy of the Dream, there is no time and no matter, there is just the 'Dream of Life.' The 'Dream' is placed on the Wheel in the Southwest, between Earth and Water.

Eight is the number of cycles and circles, pattern and repetition, physical laws. It is the 'form' of the 'dream.' Eight is the number for the Natural Law of the Universe, for Karma – the power of action-brings-reaction – which maintains balance and harmony in all things. Eight is placed in the Northwest between earth and air.

Nine is the number for Movement and Change. It is the number for Sister Moon who moves the tides and winds of

Earth, and moves the tidal waves of blood within all living beings who have hearts and the power of movement. Nine is placed Northeast between air and fire.

Ten is the number for Pure Intellect and Measure of all material things. It is the power of Movement and Change (9) plus the Light (1). Ten is the number for our Spirit-Twin or Higher-Self. The ten is placed to the north of the center of the wheel.

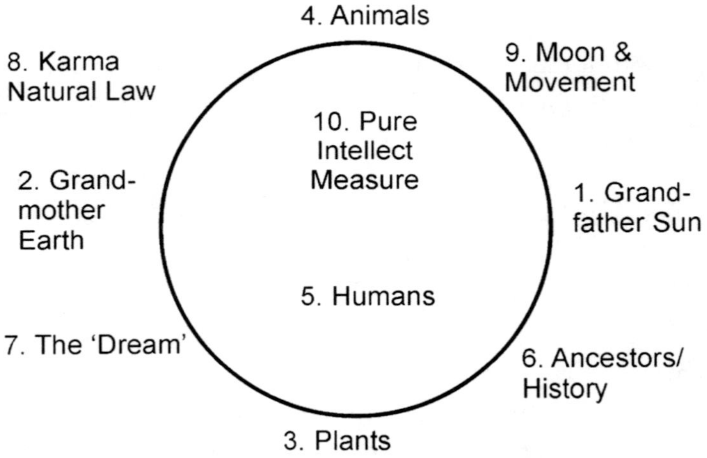

(See *Lightning Bolt* by Hyemeyohsts Storm and *A View Through The Medicine Wheel* by Leo Rutherford for more of these teachings.)

This is a small part of a much bigger teaching of the powers of the Universe and how they interact to create the reality we experience. Like all pre-patriarchal religion, they show that All comes from Oneness, Unity.

THERE IS NO SEPARATION.
GOD = CREATOR-CREATION

~ ~ ~

Judaism, Christianity, Islam and all of the male dominated religions of the last 6,000 or so years, have taken a disastrous turn away from the ancient understanding of how it is. They have made a separation of their 'God' from creation so He (not she, no balance of forces, just masculine only, thank you) has become Santa Claus for grown-ups, the god-chap.

So now let's pose the magic question: *What does (your) god create the universe out of?*

I have been told, "The ether," "He just does … out of nothing," and, "He doesn't need anything to create out of."

Okay, so if He creates out of 'nothing,' where is God now?

And, if He creates out of the ether, who was around before to create the ether? A more primal God must have been around first, so he isn't the real god at all.

If you think this through, God the True-ALL-MIGHTY can only create out of Him/Her/It-Self. For God to be ALL-MIGHTY and ABSOLUTE, there can be no thing, no energy, no consciousness, no one and nothing else around – or by definition, s/he/it isn't All-Mighty! Now when you read Genesis, you find there were lots of other people around than just the ones in the Garden of Eden. Cain even went off and married one! So it is absolutely clear that the god-chap-Jehovah is just a minor bit-player and not even mighty, never mind all-mighty.

The real God creates out of Him/Her/Itself and once you understand that the real God can only create creation out of Its-Self because that is all-there-is, then you realize that:

GOD IS WHAT WE LIVE IN AND WHAT LIVES THROUGH US.
THERE IS NO SEPARATION BETWEEN CREATOR AND THE CREATION
GOD IS THE CREATION. GOD IS EVERYTHING EVERYWHERE
AND YOU AND I LIVE INSIDE GOD.

And that changes everything! Volumes of complicated 'theology' – like all that Aruis vs Athenasius stuff trying to prove whether Jesus is or isn't god or is equal or not quite equal and all that, can go in the garbage can.

Matthew Fox, the ex-Catholic priest, ex-fellow of the Dominican order, and originator of a spiritual movement he calls 'Creation Spirituality,' in his *Ninety-five Theses* states in Thesis 4: *"God the punitive father is not a God worth honoring but a false god and an idol that serves empire builders. The notion of a punitive all-male god is contrary to the full nature of the Godhead who is as much female and motherly as it is masculine and fatherly."*

And in Thesis 6, he states: *"Theism (the idea that God is out there or above and beyond the universe) is false. All things are in God and God is in all things."*

No wonder the church threw him out! He talks sense!

In the words of Nobel Prizewinner Erwin Schrodinger: *"The overall number of minds is just one. I venture to call it indestructible since it has a peculiar timetable, namely mind is always now."*

The Universe is ONE and each of us is a cell in it. So when we make war on each other, we are like cells of the same being trying to destroy itself! Stupid? I prefer a stronger term.

I was watching a fascinating TV documentary recently about black holes and the Big Bang. Physicist Stephen Hawking's idea is that the Universe ends in a gigantic black hole where everything is swallowed up into a singularity – a point where everything becomes nothing – and then explodes back into creation from the same point. I can imagine atheists having a field day saying that proves there is no god while religionists defend themselves saying, "Oh no, it's God who makes it go bang into creation." To the shamans of the earth cultures, there is nothing to discuss. The singularity *is* the Creator, as is the Big Bang and the black hole and all of creation in between!

Many people ask, "How can a Loving-God countenance all the suffering in the world?" But the world is set up on the basis of opposites. How can you describe 'good' except in terms of 'bad'? How can you know love without knowing betrayal, abandonment and things that are not-love? How can anyone be a hero or heroine without a villain to overcome? Without both 'good' and 'bad,' there is no story, no opportunity, no development. The Chinese have it right, as their word for 'opportunity' is the same as the word for 'crisis.' Both go together.

Have you read the wonderful stories of Harry Potter? (If not, substitute your own hero/ine.) Consider the new book about Harry (or adapt for your preferred hero/ine). It begins with the death of the dastardly villain, Lord Voldemort, on page one. Then all the dodgy Slytherins (oh, what a lovely name!) decide to go straight and Harry has a wonderful gentle and rather eventless year at Hogwarts with everything going well and it is all fun and games and honesty and love and truth and – well, nothing very challenging happens at all. Not a good seller and the movie people wouldn't buy it. No challenge, no suspense, not much of a story, bit of a let-down. Fortunately not true either! I'm looking forward as much as anyone to the final book and the denouement!

God, the Real-One that is ALL-THAT-IS, has set up this planetary existence as a challenging, learning place for the many aspects of Him/Her/Itself that inhabit it. We don't and can't know all the whys and wherefores but we can speculate and do our best to learn. Some of our ancestors called God the 'Great Mystery' and that surely describes it well. Each of us is a part of it and is here to learn and grow and develop. No one can die for your 'sins' = your life problems and challenges, and no amount of 'belief' will save you from reaping the rewards of how you live your life. This is often called karma, meaning the life lessons we are here to learn. We live in a hall of mirrors and life is forever reflecting our-self to our-Self. The challenge is to stop, listen, see and feel what is being reflected. That is personal growth and is what we are here for. How does THE WHOLE – i.e., GOD – grow and develop? *Through us!* We are experiencers of The Great Mystery, experiencing it from within. As in their different ways are the animals, the birds, the plants, the insects, the planets, the suns – everything in its own way lives and experiences its Self as a form of life. The Great Mystery experiences all that within Its Body which is the Universe.

That paints a different picture to the venomous biblical god-chap, doesn't it? Which one makes more sense to you?

How much better to try to understand each other, to co-operate instead of compete, to live together in harmony rather than try to exterminate each other, to stop believing stupid, fundamentalist, literalist, religious, god-chap nonsense. We're going to have to anyway because if we don't and we set off our WMD toys, there won't be much left for anyone or of anyone.

The human race at the moment is collectively like a paranoid schizophrenic who is so determined he is right and is so terrified of others with different skins, ideas and beliefs, that he thinks they are all out to get him, so he seeks to exterminate them first and be the last living being. All alone.

Alone is safe!

But that was the condition of Great Spirit prior to Creation!

Great-Spirit was alone – which is also ALL-ONE.

And Great-Spirit chose to create a matrix of apparent reality to play in so as to learn to co-operate and to love and to grow.

Yes, this is the arena in which God Grows.

Planet Earth is GOD'S GROWTH GROUP!

With GOD as All the Participants.

It's a joke, folks, a big, fucking, cosmic joke

and it's on us.

It's WAKE-UP-OR-DIE time!

Chapter 9

It's Happening Again, so Watch Out – Another Lot Are Trying to Get Control!

"When I, or people like me, are running the country, you'd better flee, because I will find you, we will try you, and we will execute you. I mean every word of it. I will make it part of my mission to see to it that they are tried and executed .... If we're going to have true reformation in America, it is because men once again, if I may use a worn out expression, have righteous testosterone flowing through their veins. The are not afraid of contempt for their contemporaries. They are not here to get along. **They are here to take over."**

— *Randall Terry, founder of Operation Rescue, addressing a banquet sponsored by the US Tax Payers Alliance, August 8, 1995. (Operation Rescue is a US anti-abortion organisation)*

Well, Mr. Terry, that is nice and clear. When you and your kin *take over*, God help the rest of us, we will be back in the Dark Ages and the Unholy Inquisition. This is 21st century America folks, not biblical times.

Here he is again, quoted in the *Fort Wayne News Sentinel* of August 16, 1993:

"I want you to just let a wave of intolerance wash over you. I want you to let a wave of hatred wash over you. Yes, hate is good .... Our goal is a Christian nation. We have a biblical duty; we are called by God to conquer this country."

Sounds just like the Old Testament 'god-chap', doesn't he? Just as virulent, foul, bigoted, intolerant, domineering, full of hate and venom. I wonder what sort of love-life and mothering he had that left him hating so much. And isn't that a funny sort of 'Christian Country' he wants? Most Christian people talk about a loving, caring, sharing way of living, even if they are confused that they are supposed to include all people and not just fellow Christians. Still, at least he leaves no doubt about what he's aiming at.

"What you are going to hear is God's word to the men of this nation. We are going to war as of tonight. We have divine power that is our weapon. We will not compromise. Whatever truth is at risk, in the schools or legislature, we are going to contend for it. We will win ... take the nation for Jesus Christ."

— Bill McCartney. (Another right wing protagonist)

Next is a fabulous bit of rationalization from Christian Reconstuctionist Gary North, taken from *The Sinai Strategy: Economics and the Ten Commandments* (p.214):

"It occurs to me: Was Moses arrogant and unbiblical when he instructed the Israelites to kill every Canaanite in the land (Deut 7:2 and 20:16-17 – and see Chapter 3*). Was he an elitist or (horror of horrors) a racist? No; he was a God-fearing man who sought to obey God, who commanded them to kill them all. It sounds like a 'superior attitude' to me. Of course, Christians have been given no comparable military command in New Testament terms, but I am trying to deal with the attitude*

of superiority – a superiority based on our possession of the law of God. That attitude is something Christians must have when dealing with all Pagans. God has given us the tools of dominion."

My God (I invoke the real one, not the imposter god-chap), that is almost unspeakable in its superior attitude. We the Christians have the right to kill who we choose, we have the right to dominion = domination over everyone else because the god-chap gave it us. It is like the worst horrors of the Old Testament and the Inquisition coming back to haunt the 21st century.

Here he is again writing in *Backward Christian Soldiers:*

"Christians are supposed to love each other. Communists are supposed to share bonds with all proletarians and other communists. Every ideological group proclaims universality, and all of them bicker internally, never displaying unity except in the face of a common enemy. Humanism today is the common enemy of Christians."

Yes, Christians are supposed to love each other and – if we take the words of their master Jesus seriously – every one else, too – unconditionally. And yes, every ideological group bickers and guess what – Christians are incredibly good at that, too. How many Christian sects are there? I remember reading a figure quoted over 4,800 some years ago. Just as at the beginning with Arius and Athanasius (see Chapter 4) and in the world of Islam with the Sunnis and the Shias, they bicker and make war on each other. Then he calls the humanists the enemy of Christians. Why? Are they not sufficiently brainwashed? Might they talk sense and influence Christians to think for themselves? If too many people actually think for themselves, wherefore religion?

In another revealing piece from *Backward Christian Soldiers*, he says:

"The battle for the mind, some fundamentalists believe, is between fundamentalism and the institutions of the left. This conception of the battle is fundamentally incorrect. The battle for the mind is between the Christian Reconstruction Movement, which alone among Protestant groups takes seriously the Law of God, and everyone else."

Aah, so it isn't the humanists who are the real enemy. It's all the other Protestant Christian groups! And what about the Catholics, I wonder? Are they on board (doubt it) or are they enemy, too?

"We are to make Bible-obeying disciples of anybody that gets in our way."

So said Jay Grimstead in February 1987, the above quoted in *America's Taliban* by David W Irish (highly recommended).

No messing – 'we *make* them bible-obeying.' The god-chap's representatives love a bit of force now and again when their god isn't busy telling people to kill each other.

Here is Pat Robertson – remember him? He ran for president of the USA in 1984, but fortunately lost by so big a margin he didn't try again and nor have any other TV evangelists.

"There will never be world peace until God's house and God's people are given their rightful place of leadership at the top of the world."

Translation: Until we have got domination and can tell everyone else what to do, we won't let there be any peace. And to rub it in clearly, he goes on:

"The strategy against the American radical left should be the same as Gen. Douglas MacArthur employed against the Japanese in the Pacific …. Bypass their strongholds, then surround them, isolate them, bombard them, then blast the individuals out of their power bunkers with hand to hand combat. The battle for Iwo Jima was not pleasant but our troops won it. The battle to regain the soul of America won't be pleasant either, but we will win it."

— Pat Robertson's *Perspective*, April-May 1992.

Translation: We will force our beliefs on America regardless of the cost. Sounds ever more like the Old Testament. Violence, threat, war, domination, hate, killing .... Is this really what we all want in the 21st century? Is this the loving, caring religion of 'gentle Jesus'? No, it's what is hidden under the surface of this world domination cult. And it is here in the 21st century alive and kicking in America today.

Here is Pat Robertson again with a little piece of truth:

"I know there are some Christians who believe that war and their participation in it are morally wrong. While I respect their views and must allow them to follow their consciences, I do not believe the Bible teaches pacifism."

Well, he is right about that! It doesn't! Just read it for yourself. And Gary North leaves no doubt that he wants to be in control:

"The long term goal of Christians in politics should be to gain ***exclusive control over the franchise***. (My emphasis. At least the guy states his agenda clearly, terrifying as it is.) *Those who refuse to submit publicly to the eternal sanctions of God* (that means Gary and Co, folks) *by submitting to His Church's public marks of the covenant – baptism and holy communion – must be denied citizenship, just as they were in ancient Israel."*

Wow! You can see what would happen if the rightwing Christians really got power in America. Oh, what's that you say? They already have? Mr. G. W. Bush and his crew. Oh, is that why America is on such a self-destruct mission with its spurious oil wars in Iraq and Afghanistan, its monstrous debt to the rest of the world and its paranoid politicians?

And here's Gary again advocating a touch of stealth in pushing their agenda:

"So let us be blunt about it: we must ***use the doctrine of religious liberty*** *to gain independence for Christian schools until we train*

up a generation of people who know there is no religious neutrality, no neutral law, no neutral education, and no neutral civil government. Then they will get busy in constructing a Bible-based social, political and religious order which ***finally denies the religious liberty*** *of the enemies of God."* (Again - my emphasis)

So he wants to use democratic freedom to get power so he can do away with democratic freedom, just like so many scheming dictators and power thirsty psychopaths. And in the words of R.J Rushdooney:

"(We seek to) replace the heresy of democracy with Biblical law."

Rushdooney was a Calvinist (remember Calvin? – see Chapters 3 and 6) and is the 'godfather' of Christian Reconstructionism. (Quote from *America's Taliban.*)

So for this bunch of 'Christians,' democracy is a heresy. Well, of course. It stops them taking over and dominating everyone and returning the world to the Dark Ages of ignorance, poverty of spirit, the horrors of Old Testament law, the burning of books, the limitation of knowledge, the crushing of the soul, the forced uniformity of thinking, the brainwashing of the masses, the reduction of everyone else to their level of putrid, pathetic, hate-filled, paranoid, psychopathic existence.

And how about this? They even say Jesus was a killer:

"The significance of Jesus Christ as the 'faithful and true witness' is that He not only witnesses against those who are at war against God, but ***He also executes them."***

So says R.J.Rushdooney in *The Institutes of Biblical Law* (p.574) (also quoted in *America's Taliban*).

And how about this recent offering from Charles Stanley, the former two-time president of the Southern Baptist Convention and close ally of former President George Bush (senior) and fervent supporter of the current war on Iraq:

*"The government is **ordained by God** with the right to promote good and restrain evil. This includes wickedness that exists within the nation, as well as any wicked persons or countries that threaten foreign nations ... Therefore, a government has biblical grounds to go to war in the nation's defense or to liberate others in the world who are enslaved."*

Stanley warned that those who oppose or disobey the U.S. government in its drive to war *"will receive condemnation upon themselves."*

Stanley is pastor at Atlanta's First Baptist Church, a 15,000-member congregation, and is the founder of In Touch Ministries, which claims to broadcast his sermons in 14 languages to every country in the world, and which, according to Americans United for Separation of Church and State, has $40 million in assets.

Here is Pat Robertson again, from *The New World Order*, 1991:

"When I said during my presidential bid that I would only bring Christians and Jews into the government, I hit a firestorm. 'What d'you mean?' the media challenged me. 'You're not going to bring atheists into the government? How dare you maintain that those who believe the Judeo-Christian values are better qualified to govern America than Hindus and Muslims?' My simple answer is, 'Yes, they are.'"

Notice how he pits Christians and Jews as believers against Hindus and Moslems as atheists (which they are not), rather than the harder to attack humanitarians and reasonable people who want to keep the separation of church and state so that doctrinaire beliefs are kept out.

And note this, also from Pat (Op-Ed column in *USA Today*, June 2, 1994):

"The First Amendment guarantees freedom **of** *religion, not freedom* **from** *religion."*

Well, that says it all! In America, they have carte blanche to push it down your throat, no matter what! Here is a little piece from *The New World Order* (1991) where, unwittingly, he may have tumbled on a deeper truth:

"Indeed, it may well be that men of goodwill like Woodrow Wilson, Jimmy Carter and George Bush (he means sr.*), who sincerely want a larger community of nations living at peace in our world, are in reality unknowingly and unwittingly carrying out the mission and mouthing the phrases of a tightly knit cabal whose goal is nothing less than a new order for the human race under the domination of Lucifer and his followers."*

There are an increasing number of people who are very concerned that, under all the surface politics, this is exactly what is really happening. We can all see that terrorism is the excuse to vastly increase surveillance on citizens in both America and Britain, and much of Europe, too. The horrible Orwellian vision many concerned people have is that this cabal of mega-rich families, usually referred to as the 'Illuminati,' will, in years to come, have us all electronically tagged and photographed, create a financial crisis which will enable money to be replaced by 100% electronic – and therefore checkable – transactions, have us all medicated into a comfortable tranquilized state of semi-consciousness and whose ultimate aim that the human race should live as pawns in a controlled, restricted, overseen, totalitarian one-world state – just like *The Matrix*, only much worse. Such a killing of the human spirit is worth struggling against but it is worth reflecting that quite a lot of Europe has already experienced such a condition when living under the Unholy Inquisition. We have already had times like this, only it was not world-wide. And the dominators have nearly lost their greatest ally – religion – which no longer has the 'god-given' right to 'cleanse' the world of those who don't agree with it.

Heyeokah Guru says again: *God save us all from religion.*

"Today, every inhabitant of this planet must contemplate the day when this planet may no longer be inhabitable. Every man, woman and child lives under a nuclear sword of Damocles, hanging by the slenderest of threads, capable of being cut at any moment by accident or miscalculation or madness."

— John F. Kennedy, early 1960s. Assassinated.

And now forward to 2003:

"This coming battle, if it materializes, represents a turning point in USA foreign policy and possibly a turning point in the recent history of the world. This nation is about to embark upon the first test of a revolutionary doctrine applied in an extraordinary way at an unfortunate time. ***The doctrine of pre-emption – the idea that the US or any other nation can legitimately attack a nation that is not imminently threatening but may be threatening in the future*** *– is a radical new twist on the traditional idea of self-defense. It appears to be in contravention of international law and the UN charter. And it is being tested at a time of world-wide terrorism, making many countries around the globe wonder if they will soon be on our - or some other nations – hit list."*

— US Senator Robert Byrd, speaking in the US Senate 12.2.03, (quoted in *Rogue Nation* by Vernon Coleman, Blue Books, 2003.)

And here are interesting statements about the Iraq war:

"In 2003 the UN didn't need to send weapons inspectors into Iraq to find out what weapons Saddam Hussein had. All the UN needed to do was to ask the British and American Governments for an inventory. It was the British and American Governments who provided Iraq with its weapons. (Some had been gifts and some had been sold.)"

"We can say unequivocally that the industrial infrastructure needed by Iraq to produce nuclear weapons has been eliminated."

— Scott Ritter, former UN weapons inspector, before the destruction of Iraq (from *Rogue Nation*)

War and Money

Here's some scary stuff from financial expert Clif Droke, May 17, 2006 (www.clifdroke.com):

"... it has long been known by our nation's leaders that war is primarily a tool for achieving economic gain and not, as in the days of old, for territorial gains. Senator John M. Thurston of Nebraska made this infamous statement just before the Spanish American War: ***'War with Spain would increase the business and earnings of every American railroad, it would increase the output of every American factory, it would stimulate every branch of industry and domestic commerce.'***

'More recently, to end the 2000-2003 bear market and recession it was deemed necessary for the U.S. to invade Afghanistan and Iraq. Although these actions were successful in lifting the U.S. from its financial malaise, it also had the spin-off effect of escalating commodities prices, particularly the above mentioned metals and petroleum prices. This leads us to the conundrum of ***how the current inflationary environment will be addressed by the financial controllers. Specifically, will it require a further escalation of military activities (war with Iran?).*** *Or will it require a respite in military activities for a while and a corresponding slowdown in money creation to temporarily cool off commodities prices? The coming 3-4 months will reveal the answer...."*

Thank you, Clif.

NOW FOR THE WORST NIGHTMARE WE ALL FACE: 'THE RAPTURE'

The Rapture

Armageddon and the most extremist fundamentalist Christians:

The ultimate worst danger to all of us on Earth is posed by those utter abysmal lunatic fanatics who think the god-chap will bring about the 'rapture' of all fundamentalist Christians – of their particular sect, of course, no one else – when Armageddon comes. The 'rapture' is the idea that suddenly all 'true believers' (in the 'right beliefs' *only*, of course) will be bodily lifted off the planet up to 'heaven' while the rest of us have to cope with whatever shambles is left. This means the believers need have no concern for the welfare of the earth, no concern for the welfare of other humans who don't share their beliefs, no concern for the animals (after all, the Church says they don't have souls), no concern for the plants, insects, indeed for the planet herself. This is the ultimate of a destructive belief system and represents a considerable danger to the vast majority of us. It is like suicide bombing only on a massive scale. One suicide bomber takes relatively few people, animals and buildings with him, but frightened fundamentalist maniacs looking for 'rapture' will be content to take the whole planet with them.

Heyeokah says: *God save us all from 'believers.'*

This big surge of domination going on by the religious right and the so called neo-conservatives in the USA is making a right old mess around the world. At least, from the point of peace, prosperity and a good life with a healthy degree of freedom and responsibility, it is. Instead, we are getting increasing wars abroad and big-brother style restrictions on liberty and justice for ordinary people at home. However there is another big problem at the core of things:

WESTERN WORLD DEBT:

Western World Debt

Total USA recognized debt is reckoned to be over $8 trillion, which amounts to **$133,108 per family.** Every hour of every single day, the United States continues to rack up another $80 million of debt.

USA Today (October 4, 2004 – that's 2 years ago plus) reported: *"US taxpayers have a* ***bidden debt*** *of at least $53 trillion in government obligations, mostly from Medicare, Social Security and the federal debt. This debt equals* ***$473,456 per household,***

Not even the inflated value of houses will cover that. Technically it's called bankruptcy!

In the UK it is somewhat similar:

Average household debt in the UK is approximately **£47,866 including mortgages**.

Average **owed by every UK adult is approximately £25,364**. Average consumer borrowing via credit cards, motor and retail finance deals, overdrafts and unsecured personal loans has risen **to £4,107 per average UK adul**t at the end of March 2006. This has grown 52% in 5 years.

Britain's personal debt is increasing by approx £1 million every four minutes.

Britain's national debt is £1,182 billion – more than the debt of all African and South American countries put together! Over 200,000 people owe upwards of £50,000 on credit cards and around 20,000 are expected to go bankrupt in the first quarter of 2006. (Source: Credit Action)

Here is a staggering cover story (*USA Today*, November 14, 2005) quoting David Walker, the US Comptroller General:

"The United States can be likened to Rome before the fall of the empire. Its financial condition is 'worse than advertised'… It has a 'broken business model' and faces deficits in its budgets, its balance of payments, its savings - and its leadership."

And from a broader perspective:

"Whenever destroyers appear among men, they start by destroying money; for money is man's protection and the base of a moral existence. Destroyers seize gold and leave to its owners a counterfeit pile of paper. This kills all objective standards and delivers men into the arbitrary power of an arbitrary setter of values. Gold is an objective value, an equivalent of wealth produced. Paper is a mortgage on wealth that does not exist, backed by a gun aimed at those who are expected to produce it. Paper is a check drawn by legal looters upon an account which is not theirs: upon the virtue of the victims. Watch for the day when it bounces, marked, 'Account Overdrawn.'"

— Ayn Rand from Atlas Shrugged (1957)

SOMETHING IS WRONG, FOLKS.
THE FIGURES SIMPLY DO NOT ADD UP,
NOT NO-HOW.

And here are a few more interesting quotes to sum up:

"Our scientific power has outrun our spiritual power. We have guided missiles and misguided men."

— Martin Luther King

Or put it this way:

"It's amazing I won. I was running against peace, prosperity and incumbency."

— George W. Bush speaking to Swedish PM Goran Persson, unaware the live TV camera was still on!

Or this:

"It is a strange desire, to seek power, and to lose liberty; or to seek power over others, and to lose power over a man's self."

— Francis Bacon (1561-1626), British philosopher, essayist, statesman

And this from James Paul Warburg (1896-1969), while speaking before the United States Senate, February 17, 1950. He is the son of Paul Moritz Warburg, nephew of Felix Warburg and of Jacob Schiff, both of Kuhn, Loeb & Co. which poured millions into the Russian Revolution through James' brother Max, banker to the German government:

"We shall have World Government, whether or not we like it. The only question is whether World Government will be achieved by conquest or consent."

A voice of the Illuminati perhaps, who and whatever they are, are not at all illumined, just a gang of mega-rich would-be world dominators. Interesting, Huh?

The framers of the U.S. Constitution feared if their country 'fell prey' to Central Banking, they would lose power over their own ability to rule. It seems President Wilson ***recognized his own folly*** within three years of passing legislation that created the Federal Reserve:

"I have unwittingly ruined my country. A great industrial nation is controlled by its system of credit. Our system of credit is concentrated. The growth of the nation, therefore, and all our activities are in the hands of a few men. We have come to be one of the worst ruled, ***one of the most completely controlled and dominated governments in the civilized world - no longer a government by free opinion, no longer a government by conviction and the vote of the majority, but the government by the opinion and duress of small groups of dominated men."*** (My emphasis.)

Controlled and dominated - and that's the government!

And that was in 1913!

WHO ON EARTH IS RUNNING THE USA SHOW NOW?

Chapter 10

Spirituality without Religion

Essential differences between spirituality and religion:

RELIGION	**SPIRITUALITY**
Belief in One God	Trust In Existence
God Is Separate	God Is Everything
Set Of Specific Beliefs	Set Of Tools To Discover Knowledge
God is good, Devil is evil	Good and evil are two aspects of creation
Priests elected by hierarchy	Spiritual teachers / shamans accepted through ability
Repetitive dogma	Structure constantly tested by 'what works'
Masculine principal dominant	Feminine and masculine principles equal

In the ways of the ancient cultures, it was understood that God – the underlying creative force of the world – was expressed in nature, so if one wanted to learn about God, all one had to do was study nature. Remember nature includes everything that exists. It was by observation and study of 'what is' that our ancestors figured out much of how things actually work. They did not turn these findings into rigid belief systems that had to be defended against other ideas but rather treated them as understandings that could be deepened as more knowledge became revealed. Here is a quote from Thom Hartmann from his book *The Last Hours of Ancient Sunlight:*

"Older cultures, with few exceptions, hold as their most foundational concept the belief (I prefer the word understanding) *that we are not different from, separate from, in charge of, superior to, or inferior to the natural world. We are part of it. Whatever we do to nature we do to ourselves."*

Looked at in this light, it is amazing that we have replaced such ancient wisdom with belief in a 'Bible,' and other patriarchal 'holy' books, full of extraordinary contradictions and a concept of a God that is so far from an expression of love, light and truth. The result is we have a culture of wars, domination of the many by the few, 'ownership' of vast amounts of land and wealth by a relative few, millions starving while food is wasted and dumped, pollution and global warming, a crazy sex 'industry' (what a contradiction that is) fueled by all the frustration and guilt promoted for centuries by patriarchal religions, billions spent on 'defense' against other 'ourselves,' weapons of mass destruction which, if used, will terminate a substantial mass of humanity and ravage our planet. If anyone feels they can convince me we live in a sane world, please go ahead and try. Meanwhile here are some devastating conclusions from Acharya S. (The Christ Conspiracy p.415):

"In reality, Christianity was the product of a multinational cabal composed of members of a variety of brotherhoods, secret societies, and mystery schools, and was designed to empower and enrich such individuals and to unify their empire. To do so, these conspirators took myriad myths and rituals of virtually all the known cultures and combined them into one, producing a god-man to beat them all. This unreachable fictional

character had since been considered the 'greatest man who ever walked the earth,' to whom no one else can compare and besides whom no one else deserves much recognition and appreciation. All others are, in fact, pathetic born-in-sin wretches. But he did not walk the earth, and we must hereafter allow the dignity of sanctity to be bestowed upon not just one 'man' but all of creation."

And Lloyd Graham writing in *Deceptions and Myths of the Bible* (Citadel, 1991):

"Such a story as the gospels tell us is unworthy of man's respect; it is, we repeat, the greatest fraud and hoax ever perpetrated upon mankind."

So looking at this fraud and hoax from a more personal level, how has it hurt and damaged individuals of the present time? What beliefs do many people hold that keep their souls crushed so much smaller than they could be? What hardships and misery has this fraud brought to masses of people over the last two millennia? What is the deep seated anguish and neuroses of the cultures that still live under the brainwashed belief in the god-chap, under the myth of expulsion from the Garden of Eden?

The first is *lousy self-esteem.* I have heard that the Dalai Lama, when addressing a meeting of American Psychotherapists, asked them for the prime reason people sought their services. Their reply was: 'lack of self-esteem.' The Dalai Lama's response was 'What's that?'

Not all cultures suffer the same complaints, but how can people of a culture that holds a collective belief of rejection by its God and expulsion out of God's Garden possibly hold themselves in esteem? No way. So the first pain of Christianized people is directly the result of cockeyed religious teaching. If you feel deep down that you are rejected and abandoned by God, what do you do? The chances are one of three things:

1. Live in your head, avoiding emotional pain, rationalizing, logicalizing, and then competing or warring against others to 'prove' yourself.
2. Live destructively with drugs, indulgence, unloving sex, fights and so on.
3. Become a fundamentalist clinging for dear life to The Group who are RIGHT and have the ONLY TRUTH. Perhaps you'll even fantasize the 'rapture' when you will be amongst the 'CHOSEN ONES' and you'll go straight to 'heaven,' do not pass go, do not collect $200! And won't that just show 'em!

The second big issue is *fear*. Again, the teaching that one should 'fear God' is a travesty. Respect the enormity and power of existence, yes, but cringe in fear? Fear the result of one's own egoism and selfishness – yes. Fear the periodic eruptions of nature – yes. But fear most the violent, condemning, imposter-god-chap, and especially fear the world-dominating antics of his 'true believers.'

The third is *shame and guilt*. The absurd teachings of the biblical god-chap that the body is an unworthy and unholy vehicle for spirit leads to inner war, yourself against yourself. The insane anti-sexual teachings make any normal person feel shame and guilt just because they are normal, as I hope I have shown graphically in earlier chapters.

The fourth is the *defiling and denigration of woman* and the imbalance created between the rights of women and men. Woman has been made a second class citizen, and in some eras, more like a chattel for the use and abuse of men.

The fifth is *belief* itself. One of my teachers many years ago expressed it as to: *'BE-in-the-LIE, and what you then get begins with F.....!'*

Heyeokah says: *Belief is the greatest enemy of knowledge.*

And I am not alone in this:
"The greatest enemy of the truth is not lies but firmly held beliefs."
— Schopenhauer

"Belief, in fact, is every human's greatest foe. More people have believed what life is than people who have learned what life is."
— Estcheemah (shamaness) quoted by Hyemeyhosts Storm in *Lightningbolt* (p.267)

'The devil,' in the shape of people without integrity, is out there in myriad disguises saying believe-in-me, trust-in-us, give us your power, let me make up your mind for you, let me sign your checks or better still just give me your checkbook to look after; surrender to me – a spiritual master – worship at my one true altar; the 'only son of god' is our property and unless you worship with us, you are doomed; we are god's holy chosen people and anyone who crosses us is an enemy of god (so convenient); we bring the 'one true god' to the heathens and, until they are converted, they are subhuman so it is our right and duty to conquer them, take their lands, enslave them and 'save' them – all for their own good, of course.

Belief has been peddled in so many ways, but belief beggars any possibility of real knowledge, growth and wisdom. The very act of becoming 'a believer' is an act of being-in-a-lie, of saying, "I will close my mind to any further information which conflicts with this dogma I have chosen to accept." Believing without knowledge is 'selling your soul to the devil.' It gives you the poison of 'absolute certainty' from which you can attack all who see differently.

This poisonous certainty, this 'being-in-the-lie' prevents any connection with the real Creator in which we and all living things exist as co-creators, as aspects of Creation. The price is nothing less than your freedom – and people everywhere seem to be looking for something or someone to pay this diabolical price to. Anything to save them from the deeply humbling journey to self-knowledge, the enormous challenge of self-responsibility, of making and standing by their own choices and reaping the benefits or otherwise, the responsibility and right to create and live their own lives in their own way, the right to explore and learn through experience just what really is and is not.

LET ME MAKE SOMETHING CLEAR ABOUT BELIEF AND/OR FAITH:

A lot of people talk about faith when they actually mean belief. Faith means trust in the Universe, in Existence, in one's Inalienable Right to Exist as part of this incredible Existence, this fantastic vast unfathomable glorious Universe. However, the moment one postulates a separate god-figure who is somewhere else and supposedly created the Universe yet is somehow separate from it, one is into the realm of fantasy and belief, of 'being-in-the-lie.' Faith is about trust in existence, in the miracle of being. To have FAITH is an essential for health, hope, happiness, harmony and all such good things and places oneself firmly within the Goodness of All Creation. To be-lie-ve in just one specific concept of God and just one 'right' way of relating to God / Creation and make all other ways wrong is to separate oneself, sit in judgement and create loneliness and isolation.

"There is no doubt that, at this moment in history, Western Civilization is suffering from a great sickness of the soul. The West's progressive turning away from functioning spiritual values; its total disregard for the environment and the protection of natural resources; the violence of inner

cities with their problems of poverty, drugs and crime; spiraling unemployment and economic disarray; and growing intolerance toward people of color and values of other cultures – all of these trends, if unchecked, will eventually bring about a terrible self-destruction. In the face of all this global chaos, the only possible hope is self-transformation."

— Malidoma Patrice Some, PhD., Dagara Medicine Man of Burkina Faso, from *Of Water and the Spirit*

EXACTLY! SELF-TRANSFORMATION!

Not infantile beliefs that some god-chap or 'His Son' will do it all for us.

'Being-in-the-lie' – the real human problem is our willingness and proclivity to believe without knowledge.

You might feel that this book is a diatribe against religion but actually religion is only a symptom, it is not the problem itself. The problem is the extraordinary readiness of much of the human race to 'BE-IN-THE-LIE' – the propensity we have to believe what we are told, to take on board what others tell us, to be vulnerable to advertising, coercion, persuasion – in a word – brainwashing. So when a religion is sold to us with the aid of threats to our life, as happened around AD 150 – 400 when the burgeoning cult of Christianity turned ancient myth into literal 'fact' and was then 'nationalized' by the emperor Constantine, it was only too easy for humans to take it on board without much in the way of thought or reflection. Well, it was either that or being dead. Then, as time went by, it became accepted as the norm and millions still 'be-in-the-lie' of it, the torturous and murderous coercion of its origins having been almost totally obliterated from memory.

Let me give you a simple example of belief: 'fish on Fridays.'

Remember that? It was gospel when I grew up that godly people should eat fish on Fridays. Why? History shows that a church document of the Council of Toledo decreed in the year AD 447 that believers should abstain primarily from meat on all Fridays and on days of penance. Canon 1251 of the 1983 Code of Canon Law prescribes: *"abstinence from meat unless a solemnity should fall on a Friday."*

Then in 1563, *"for the increase of provision of fish by the more usual and common eating thereof,"* it was enacted that, under penalty of a fine or three months jail, fish should be the Friday meal. So because long, long ago fishermen were having a tough time selling their fish, everyone "of faith" had to eat fish on Fridays, *by papal decree!*

And I can attest that this idea was still prevalent in the 1940s and 1950s in England when I was growing up. And all because many centuries ago fishermen were having a hard time selling fish!

Now here is a much more horrendous result of 'being-in-the-lie': female genital mutilation.

Female genital mutilation is an appalling, destructive, invasive procedure that is part of many North and West African cultures. It predates the religions we know and to their lasting shame, neither Christianity or Islam have made any attempt to prevent it. It is usually performed on girls before puberty. Part, or all, of the clitoris is cut out and in the most extreme cases the labia are sewn up with just a small hole for menstrual blood to escape. All without anesthetic, until recently. This is an incredible trauma and it leaves women with reduced or no sexual feeling. Orgasms are often impossible to experience later in life and many health and psychological problems result from the 'surgery.' This operation is still forced on approximately 6,000 girls per day, worldwide – about one every 15 seconds.

Here is one unfortunate woman's experience verbatim:

"I was seven years old when I was excised. I recall the stories from women of my village who spoke of this operation as if their whole life had stopped there and then. The atrocity of their descriptions and at the same time a feeling of inescapable doom had triggered such a panic in me that when the terror-laden day came, I began to vomit. What happened then is still excruciatingly burning my flesh, so much so that I often wake up in the middle of the night screaming and calling for my mother."

The horrible irony to that is that her mother will have been fully complicit in the terror and pain she experienced, as it is the women who, generation by generation, do it to the women. I watched a TV program last year which showed it being done on two girls, somewhere in Africa. It was done with a local anesthetic (imagine having a needle thrust into the tenderest part of your genitals) yet it was unbelievably horrendous, especially seeing the mounting terror of the second girl to be 'done' as she saw what was happening as her sister was held down by several large women and forced into submission. It was quite dreadful to watch it but I wanted to know the truth.

Some say this practice comes from the Pharaohs, others say not. (See *Women of Omdurman* by Anne Cloudsley.) I have been unable to find out its definite origins but there is one thing I can say for certain. It comes from patriarchy, from the god-chap, from male domination and the desire of some males to reduce women to mere chattels for their pleasure and use.

And it is time for a campaign of education to help those who are still robotically committing this appalling act because of their 'be-lie-fs.'

Heyeokah's reflections on the current craziness of our society:

- For spiritual understanding – avoid the church!
- For true information – avoid newspapers!

- For real healthy food – avoid most of the usual shops and supermarkets!
- For good health – seek 'alternative' medicine and avoid most doctors and hospitals!
- For history – avoid official HIS-story and seek underground suppressed knowledge!
- For self-understanding – avoid education and psychiatry and seek the ancient knowledge of the shamans and wise people of the earth-based cultures!

Here are a few statistics which show the 'efficacy' of modern ways, from *Rogue Nation* by Vernon Coleman (Blue Books, 2003):

"It is now claimed that 200,000 Americans get food poisoning every day. Modern processed meats are said to leave more fecal bacteria on the average American kitchen sink than can be found on the average American toilet seat."

According to the Journal of the American Medical Association (JAMA), the overall incidence of serious adverse drug reaction in America is now 6.7%, while the incidence of fatal Adverse Drug Reactions is 0.32% of hospitalized patients. JAMA estimates that in one year well over two million hospitalized patients in the USA have serious Adverse Drug Reactions, while 106,000 have fatal ones. In fact, it is between the 4th and 6th leading cause of death in USA!

Note: JAMA *excluded* errors in drug administration, noncompliance, overdose, drug abuse, therapeutic failures and possible ADRs.

Every year around 100,000 Americans die of infections caught in hospital.

Another source says a total of 350,000 Americans die per annum (2005) from both properly and improperly prescribed medications and that it is now the 3rd leading cause of death.

It seems that boys in American schools who run about and shout tend to be diagnosed as hyperactive. It has been claimed that up to 12 % of all American boys of age 6-14 are on Ritalin or similar drugs!

Each year the world spends over $1 trillion on arms. The Presidential Commission on World Hunger estimated that it would cost $6 billion per year to eradicate starvation and malnutrition. That is equivalent to less that three days arms expenditure!

The USA is reckoned to be responsible for a quarter of all pollution on the planet.

> *"Our (USA) population is doubling every 40 years, environment being destroyed by the chemical leprosies of urban smog, acid rain, ozone depletion, carbon dioxide, toxic pollution. Our forests are disappearing and our deserts expanding. Some 20 million of us die slowly, painfully and needlessly of starvation each year and another 700 million go malnourished."*
>
> — *The Spirit Of Shamanism* by Roger N. Walsh (p.253)

And a new shocking world statistic: In 2006, 800 million people are malnourished, six million die each year for lack of basic necessities, and one child starves to death every five seconds.

The Empire Problem

Many male animals live in a 'fuck-or-fight' universe, one of simple power over others, of territory and battles. We humans are still quite largely living in this primitive simplicity of mind and for several millennia, since concepts of male domination swept over human society, we have created empire after empire based on just such narrow thinking. It is worthwhile noting that *every empire*, all the way from Gilgamesh to the British Empire, *has fallen!* The current 'emperors' – the Americans – are clearly approaching the end of their time right now and are behaving with reckless abandon, as have many empires before, in their death throes.

For all our advancement in the ways of science and the manipulation of material things, we are still – very sadly – an ignorant species that is an enormously long way from learning to live in co-operation and harmony with each other and our planet. We are still primitive, territorial and warlike. We have yet to develop a working-together global consciousness and it is dubious whether we will be able to do that before our destruction of the ecology of the earth dooms a large number of us to an early and unnecessary demise. This is the biggest challenge of the 21st century.

Here are some words from a very knowledgeable person: Erwin Laszlo, Ph.D., founder and president of The Club of Budapest, founder and director of the General Evolution Research Group, and editor of the international periodical *World Futures*, as well as author of 47 books. (Writing in *Caduceus Magazine*, Spring 2006)

"We are approaching a critical point in our collective evolution: our world has become economically, socially and ecologically unsustainable. Persisting in the values and practices of the rationalistic, manipulative civilization of the modern age will create deepening rifts between rich and poor, young and old, informed and marginalized, and human societies and the natural environment. To survive in our planetary home, we must create a world better adapted to the conditions we have ourselves created."

IT'S GROW-UP-OR-DIE TIME.

The God-man Story for All of Us

Jesus, as a story, an eternal myth, is infinitely stronger than the idea that he was a literal man who actually lived. A great healer may well have lived and there are stories in Kashmir of Issa who studied Buddhism there in his youth, went home to Judaea to work his mission and later returned and lived out his life, died in old age and is buried in Srinagar. There are other stories about Jesus the Rabbi who was married to Mary Magdalene. Something of this may be so and it may be that stories have got mixed together. But the Son of God myth is an eternal myth and was never meant as a literal event. It is the *Sun* of God, personalized. It is a guide for all people, 'His' life is your life in potential, 'His' story is a metaphor for your story as the events in 'His' mythological life happen in yours. Remember, a myth is something that is always true but never happened. The challenges 'He' faces in 'His' story are the same archetypal ones you face in your life.

The journey has been described in many ways by many cultures and called by many names: The Perennial Philosophy, the Search for the Holy Grail, the Buddha's search for enlightenment, the Jesus Story as understood by the Original Gnostic Christians, the Arthurian legends, the Journey of Osiris/Dionysus, the Journey into the Mind of God and so on. Here is the essence of the God-(Wo)Man's Journey:

We are all born away from our home which in the spirit world. We are born to parents who created our body-vehicle but not our spirit. They are not our real parents who are (quite literally) Father Sun (or Father Sky) and Mother Earth (Virgin Mare). Our birth is supported by spirit guides / 'angels' who assist our spirit in our early years to adapt to the body-vehicle and its environment. At around the age of twelve, we naturally tend to challenge the status quo. We go through puberty, we manifest our 'weapons of mass creation' in becoming sexual beings and we take on responsibility for our own being. We seek a job or vocation and we learn to contribute and earn our own living. Most create a family. We are tempted by the counter force, struggle with all the challenges of human life and we have to make up our own mind whether we live with integrity or not and to what extent. We are challenged by the 'cross,' the limiting and restricting powers of the four directions, the powers of earth, air, water and fire which for us are the powers of body, mind, emotions and spirit. We are challenged ultimately to die to our ego-separateness and to be 'reborn' in conscious Oneness with God-Spirit-Universe-Creation, living as part of the Great Unity of All-Things. Each one of us is the 'Christ upon the Cross' of matter and we are spirit 'crucified'/ constricted within the limitations of the body and the third dimensional world of gross matter. Our task to achieve maturity is to 'get down off the cross,' to realize that we are part of what creates this Universe and to consciously become Masters of our own Self and Co-Creators of our own Destiny.

The great mythologist Joseph Campbell says in *The Hero with 1000 Faces* (Paladin 1988 / first published 1949 by Princeton University press):

"*...religious pantomime is hardly more today than a sanctimonious exercise for Sunday morning, whereas business ethics and patriotism stand for the remainder of the week. Such a monkey-holiness is not what the functioning world requires; rather a transmutation of the whole social order is necessary, so that through every detail and act of secular life* ***the image of the universal god-man who is actually immanent and effective in all of us may somehow be made known to consciousness.***" (My emphasis.)

The Mayans say: *"In Lakech,"* meaning, "I am another yourself, you are another myself." We are all One. What we do to others, we do to aspects of our self. The answer to human life is the recognition deep inside that All-Is-One, that 'God' is The-Creation-We-Live-In-And-Are-Part-Of.

"The deepest level of truth uncovered by science and by philosophy is the fundamental truth of The Unity. At that deepest subnuclear level of our reality, you and I are literally one."

— John Hagelin PhD. Quantum physicist, from *The Little Book of Bleeps* (Revolver Books, 2004)

And in the words of Albert Einstein:

"A human being is part of the whole called by us Universe, a part limited in time and space. He experiences himself, his thoughts and feelings as something separated from the rest, a kind of optical delusion of his consciousness. This delusion is a kind of prison for us, restricting us to our personal desires and to affection for a few persons nearest to us. Our task must be to free ourselves from this prison by widening our circle of compassion to embrace all living creatures and the whole of nature and its beauty."

Knowledge:

"To know that we know what we know, and to know that we do not know what we do not know, that is true knowledge."

— Copernicus.

Heyeokah Guru's Last Word (well, it's my book!)

Firstly, just one thing: Please don't ***believe*** a word of what I say! Let my words affect you, stimulate you, move you to think and seek truth for yourself. But no more 'being-in-the-lie.' Trust only your own experience, your own truth, your own knowing. It's the only truth you've got and ever will have.

This is a bit of mine: I used to think I knew a bit. But that was when I still naively believed too much of what I was told, when I was still 'in-the-lie,' still living from the mental programs that were pushed onto me, when I was still brainwashed. Now I have thought for myself, sought, looked, sifted and lifted the covers, studied lots of things especially what those in power like to hide, I know I no longer know much. But at least the opinions I have are my own and not just regurgitated brainwashing. So, for what it is worth, this is a bit of what I think:

There was no fall, no resurrection, and no savior who did it all for us. These are aspects of our individual story: we fall from oneness with mother, we resurrect = re-create ourselves as individuals, we become our own savior and guide. We have been conned into believing in a religion and its 'god-chap' and 'only-son-chap' so as to make us powerless and dependent. We have been sold an imposter, conned into worshipping a male domination cult of violence, war, competitiveness, racism, separation and hate who teaches us to denigrate the feminine, revile the human body and ravage the earth, all with no concern except to get off to 'heaven' regardless of what catastrophe we leave behind, and with little concern for what our children will inherit. Our myths and legends have been skewed and screwed to give a toxic foundation to our society which is reflected in the dire toxic effects we are having on the earth's ecology. We have been misled to look at life in terms of either–or rather than both–and; the Newtonian version of reality rather than the Quantum version. These paradigms are redundant. It is time to change our way of thinking and being.

We become what we believe, what we hold to be true in our deepest semi and 'unconscious' mind – the part of our mind that can be most easily brainwashed. If we believe in a male-dominator war-god, that is what we become and what we create. And sadly, we see the effects all around. If we believe in an

Infinite-Creator-God of Ultimate Love and Compassion, that is what we will become and that is the very different future we will create together. It will make a start to give The Eternal Mother back her rightful place in the church's Trinity.

Many of the old cultures have legends that say this is the third world or the fourth world and that previous humanities have reached this place in evolution and a mass extinction has occurred. We can see all around us the potential for this happening again. It seems that Creation (God) has set Itself-In-Us a giant task to get past this enormous challenge. That means to wake up, to grow up, to come out of the lies, face ourselves, take responsibility for our actions and the results of those actions and look after each other in the deep knowledge that we are ultimately one.

Each of us can take steps to manifesting our High-Self / Spiritually-Connected-Self instead of living as the competitive, separated, eternally warring, egotistical human fool. Now is the time to drop the toxic beliefs with their baggage of unworthiness and to manifest the best within us, the God-Wo/Man within; to help the human world towards realization of the urgent need for sustainable living and recognition of the ecological catastrophe on our doorstep; to awaken to the madness of war; to embrace a loving, compassionate, co-operative, peaceful path of life, to become part of the solution and no longer part of the problem, to recognize we are ultimately just One Being.

Which life would you rather create? Who of your possible selves would you rather become? What future would benefit your children the most?

TIME IS RUNNING FAST —
IT'S TIME TO COME OUT-OF-THE-LIE
IT'S TIME TO WAKE UP

Sources, Resources and Recommended Reading

The Jesus Mysteries, Timothy Freke and Peter Gandy, Harper Collins – Thorsons 1999. Republished by Element 2003

Jesus and the (Lost) Goddess, same authors, Harper Collins – Thorsons 2001

The Laughing Jesus – Religious Lies and Gnostic Wisdom, same authors, Harmony Books (Random House) 2005

The Christ Conspiracy – The Greatest Story Ever Sold, Acharya S., Adventures Unlimited Press, 1999.

The Book Your Church Doesn't Want You to Read. edited by Tim C. Leedom, Kendall / Hunt Publishing Co, Iowa, USA, 1993

The Dark Side of Christian History, Helen Ellerbe, Morningstar & Lark, 1995 (seventh printing, 2004)

The Woman's Encyclopedia of Myths and Secrets, Barbara G Walker, Harper, San Francisco, 1983

When Religion Becomes Evil, Charles Kimball, 2003

The Last Hours of Ancient Sunlight, Thom Hartmann, Hodder and Stoughton, 1998

Lightningbolt, Hyemeyohsts Storm, Ballantine, 1994

A View through the Medicine Wheel, Leo Rutherford, 2007

Care of the Soul, Thomas Moore, Piatkus, 1992

The Hero with 1000 Faces, Joseph Campbell,. Paladin, 1988 (first published 1949)

Before God the Father, Mary Daly, Beacon Press, Boston, 1973

The Chalice and the Blade, Riane Eisler

Stupid White Men, Michael Moore, 2001

Rogue Nation, Vernon Coleman, Blue Books, 2003

Shamanic Path Workbook, Leo Rutherford, Arima Publications, 2006

Of Water and the Spirit, Malidoma Some, Penguin, 1994

The Spirit of Shamanism, Roger N. Walsh

Living with Soul, Vols 1 & 2, Tony Stubbs, Dandelion Books, 2006

Christianity as Mystical Fact, Rudolph Steiner, Anthroposophic Press, 1972

Sinners in the Hands of an Angry God, Jonathan Edwards, 1742

Christianity – An Ancient Egyptian Religion, Ahmed Osman

Women of Omdurman – Life, Love and the Cult of Virginity, Anne Cloudsley, *Ethnographia*, 1981/3 (re: victims of genital mutilation)

Children at Risk: The Battle for the Hearts and Minds of Our Kids, James Dobson, World Publishing, 1990

On Injure-cation

The Making of Them, Nick Duffell, Lone Arrow Press, 2000

The Old School Tie, Jonathan Gathorne-Hardy, Viking Press, New York

Dick Whippington and the Boys (and Girls) of Beaton College, Elsie-Ruth Erford, 2007

Pamphlets

Published by See Sharp Press, USA www.seesharppress.com (Highly recommended)

America's Taliban in Its Own Words, David W Irish, 2003

The Heretics Guide to the Bible, edited by Chaz Bufe, 1987

Pagan Christs, Joseph McCabe, 1999

Judeo-Christian Degradation of Women, Joseph McCabe,1998

Magazines

Nexus Magazine, 55 Queens Road, East Grinstead, West Sussex, RH19 1BG, UK

Caduceus Magazine, 9 Nine Acres, Midhurst, West Sussex, GU29 9EP, UK

Sacred Hoop, UK's shamanism/paganism magazine. Anghorfa, Abercych, Boncath, Pembrokehsire SA37 0EZ, UK

Informative Websites

www.evilbible.com (a wealth of useful info)
www.becomingachristian.com (unbelievable, simplistic crap)
http://oror.essortment.com/constantine_rbsr.htm (inforomation on Emperor Constantine)
www.skepticsannotatedbible.com/women/long.html
www.angelfire.com
http://100prophecies.org/christianity.htm
www.religionfacts.com
http://geneva.rutgers.edu/src/christianity/major.html
www.catholic.com/library/Birth_Control.asp
www.languedoc-france.info/1201_beliefs.htm
www.califmall.com/earthstarconsultingcom/aboutHDS article54.htm
www.cuttingedge.org
www.genesis.net.au/~bible/kjv/genesis/
www.dhushara.com/book/diversit/saceve.htm# anchor3147959
www.dhushara.com/book/zulu/islamp/nakface/ naked.htm#anchor205500
http://home.earthlink.net/~pgwhacker/ChristianOrigins/
www.medmalexperts.com/POCM/ triumph_over_other_Christianities.htm
www.davidicke.com/

IF YOU LIKED THIS BOOK, YOU WON'T WANT TO MISS OTHER TITLES BY DANDELION BOOKS
Available Now And Always Through *www.dandelionbooks.net* And Affiliated Websites!!
TOLL-FREE ORDERS – 1-800-861-7899 (U.S. & CANADA)

Non-Fiction – Conscious Solutions:

Living with Soul: An Old Soul's Guide to Life, the Universe and Everything, Vol. I, by Tony Stubbs... Who are we? Where did we come from? Why are we here? Master teacher and sage Tony Stubbs urges us to "go to the Source... look in the mirror." In the first of a two-volume compendium of comprehensive spiritual teachings, Stubbs expertly documents his lessons and observations with excellent anecdotes, charts and other graphics. (ISBN 1-893302-85-7) $27.95 + S & H

Living with Soul: An Old Soul's Guide to Life, the Universe and Everything, Vol. II, by Tony Stubbs... Learn how to work with energy and make it work for you by discovering your own energy patterns or bio-rhythms. Explore reincarnation, death, grief, near-death experiences, life on the "other side" and many other multi-dimensional experiences. Also learn more about the coming U.S. disclosures concerning extraterrestrials, UFOs and many over-ups that may have "Earth-shattering" repercussions for those who until now have been unwilling to accept that "we are not alone." (ISBN 1-893302-86-5) - $27.95 + S & H

Unveil the Past: Heal the Future through Hypnosis & Hypnotherapy, by Doris Small Proiette, DCH, Ph.D.... Amazing stories from Dr. Proiette's clinical records about the healing power of past life regression that reaffirms the power of the mind and the ability for every human being to release themselves from unwanted feelings and belief systems. Dr. Proiette's books supports statistics that show Hypnotherapy as the leading technology for helping people heal their issues of dis-ease and dysfunction. (ISBN 1-893302-96-2) - $21.95 ($24.50 Canada) + S&H

Portals to Higher Consciousness: Exploring the Spiritual Domain, by Norman D. Livergood... What is the process that serious students use to actually realize—bring to manifestation—their Higher Consciousness, "through which they are able to contact Reality in a region of pure Truth." If you're interested in investigating higher consciousness, put on your hiking clothes and join this spiritual expedition (1-893302-92X) $29.95 + S & H

*Creation and Metempsychosis (The Evolution of the Soul): An Introduction to the "Psychological Key of Man,"*edited and compiled by Q. Dean Sloan... A compilation of theosophical metaphysics that provides the technical metaphysical rationale for Creation itself, as well as Creation of the human soul ("crown chakra") and is based on the psychology of the 7 rays. "The 'petals' in the crown chakra unfold slowly over a long series of lives, and we achieve perfection only when they have completely unfolded." (ISBN 1-893302-90-3) $36.95 + S & H

The Perennial Tradition: Overview Of The Secret Heritage, The Single Stream Of Initiatory Teaching Flowing Through All The Great Schools Of Mysticism, by Norman D. Livergood... Like America, Awake, this book is another wake-up call. "It was written to assist readers to awaken to the Higher Spiritual World." In addition to providing a history of the Western tradition of the Perennial Tradition, Livergood also describes the process that serious students use to actually *realize*—bring to manifestation—their Higher Consciousness. "Unless we become aware of this higher state, we face the prospect of a basically useless physical existence and a future life—following physical death—of unpleasant, perhaps anguished reformation of our essence." (ISBN 1-893302-48-2) - $21.95 + S & H

Progressive Awareness: Critical Thinking, Self-Awareness & Critical Consciousness, by Norman D. Livergood... how to avoid being manipulated by our emotions and ideas and how to start thinking for ourselves; increase your skills for understanding, critical thinking, self-awareness, critical consciousness, and enlightened discernment. (ISBN 1-893302-80-6) - $19.95 + S & H

My Name is Esther Clara, by Laurel Johnson... Esther Clara's lifetime spanned two world wars and the inventions of electricity, telephones, automobiles, airplanes, radio, TV, computers and many other conveniences that have become basic necessities of modern American life. An authentic first-hand account of 20th century rural America audio and videotaped before her death and adeptly reconstituted by master storyteller and book reviewer, Laurel Johnson. (ISBN 1-893302-89-X) – 16.95 + S & H

Why Don't You Love Me? I'm the Best Choice: Repairing Heartache, Finding the Right Mate & Not Making the Same Mistakes the Next Time, by Debi Davis... Everyone has a perfect mate waiting for them and it may not be the person you are trying to hold onto now. Learn how to manifest that perfect partner... for you by clearly identifying the qualities you're looking for and making sure you show the world a true and honest portrait of who you are. (ISBN 1-893302-91-1) $12.95 + S & H

The Compassionate Surgeon, by Joop Schokker, M.D. . . . Do you or someone you love need an operation? Scared? Don't know where to turn for advice?

Let Dr. Joop Schokker guide you through the process and answer such questions as: What should you expect before, during and after surgery? What should you ask of, and expect from, your surgeon? What can go wrong and how will your surgeon fix it? When is surgery unnecessary? What are your chances of full recovery? (ISBN 0-963294-76-8) - $12.95 + S & H

Executive Parenting: Risks & Solutions for the Working Parent-What you may not know . . . but will wish you did!, by Debi Davis & Ellen Sherman, Ph.D. . . .Health expert Debi Davis and Marriage and Family Counselor Dr. Ellen Sherman have combined their knowledge and experience to deliver a comprehensive manual for child-rearing in the 21st century. (ISBN 1-893302-93-8) - $19.95 + S & H

The Courage To Be Who I Am, by Mary-Margareht Rose... This book is rich with teachings and anecdotes delivered with humor and humanness, by a woman who followed her heart and learned to listen to her inner voice; in the process, transforming every obstacle into an opportunity to test her courage to manifest her true identity. (1SBN 1-893302-13-X) - $20.95 + S & H

The Making Of A Master: Tracking Your Self-Worth, by Jeanette O'Donnal... A simple tracking method for self-improvement that takes the mystery out of defining your goals, making a road map and tracking your progress. A book rich with nuggets of wisdom couched in anecdotes and instructive dialogues. (ISBN 1-893302-36-9) - $14.95 + S & H

Non-Fiction – Uncensored and Unfettered:

Overthrow of the American Republic – The Writings of Sherman H. Skolnick, by Sherman H. Skolnick... Known as "America's leading judge-buster," the late Sherman H. Skolnick was one of America's most courageous and outrageous journalists. This collection of his internet writings also includes 24 articles that were never published on his website. This 600-page book which contains over 80 Skolnick articles, is a complement to Skolnick's *Ahead of the Parade*, published by Dandelion Books in 2003. (ISBN 1-893302-22-9)

It's All About Control: The God, Jesus and ET Cover-up Conspiracies, by Tony Stubbs... Three major conspiracies are controlling the people of planet Earth: This book provides the truth-serum and tools for breaking free from a cruel, cleverly contrived mind-control game that for centuries has been keeping the human race in bondage to the Religion, War and Finance industries. (ISBN 1-893302-95-4)

Exopolitics: Political Implications of the Extraterrestrial Presence, by Michael E. Salla, Ph.D.... According to Dr. Michael Salla and many other experts in the field of ET research, for almost 70 years the US government has engaged in an extensive "official effort" of disinformation, intimidation and tampering with evidence in order to maintain a non-disclosure policy about extraterrestrial presence. (ISBN 1-893302-56-3)

America Speaks Out: Collected Essays From Dissident Writers John H. Brand, Meria Heller, John Kaminski, Norman D. Livergood, Wayne Madsen, Kurt Nimmo, Albert D. Pastore, Michael E. Salla, Sherman H. Skolnick & John Stanton... A collection of essays extracted from works recently published by Dandelion Books. (ISBN 1-893302-63-6)

Unshackled: A Survivor's Story of Mind Control, by Kathleen Sullivan... A non-fictional account of Kathleen Sullivan's experiences as part of a criminal network that includes Intelligence personnel, military personnel, doctors and mental health professionals contracted by the military and the CIA, criminal cult leaders and members, pedophiles, pornographers, drug dealers and Nazis. "I believe my story needs to be told so that more people will understand how 'Manchurian Candidate' style mind-control techniques can create alter-states in the minds of unwitting victims, causing them to perform deeds that are normally repugnant." (ISBN 1-893302-35-0)

Shaking The Foundations: Coming Of Age In The Postmodern Era, by John H. Brand, D.Min., J.D.... Scientific discoveries in the Twentieth Century require the restructuring of our understanding the nature of Nature and of human beings. In simple language the author explains how significant implications of quantum mechanics, astronomy, biology and brain physiology form the foundation for new perspectives to comprehend the meaning of our lives. (ISBN 1-893302-25-3)

Rebuilding The Foundations: Forging A New And Just America, by John H. Brand, D.Min., J.D....Should we expect a learned scholar to warn us about our dangerous reptilian brains that are the real cause of today's evils? Although Brand is not without hope for rescuing America, he warns us to act fast– and now. Evil men intent on imposing their political, economic, and religious self-serving goals on America are not far from achieving their goal of mastery." (ISBN 1-893302-33-4)

Cancer Doctor: The Biography Josef Issels, M.D., Who Brought Hope To The World With His Revolutionary Cancer Treatment, by Gordon Thomas...Dr. Josef Issels treated more than 12,000 cancer patients who had been written off as "incurable" by other doctors. He claimed no miracle cures, but the success record of his revolutionary "whole person treatment" was extraordinary...

the story of his struggle against the medical establishment which put Dr. Issels in prison, charged with fraud and manslaughter. (ISBN 1-893302-18-0)

Fiction with Flare:

Waaaay Out There! Diggertown, Oklahoma, by Tuklo Nashoba…Adventures of constable Clint Mankiller and his deputy, Chad GhostWolf; Jim Bob and Bubba Johnson, Grandfather GhostWolf, Cassie Snodgrass, Doc Jones, Judge Jenkins and the rest of the Diggertown, Oklahoma bunch in the first of a series of Big Foot-Sasquatch tall tales peppered with lots of good belly laughs and just as much fun. (ISBN 1-893302-44-X) - $13.95 + S & H

Waaaay Out There! Arbuckle Treasure Hunt, by Tuklo Nashoba… The second in the WAAAAY OUT THERE series that takes Clint Mankiller and his deputy, Chad GhostWolf, Bubba and the rest of the Diggertown gang high up in to the Arbuckle Mountains on a hunt for buried Spanish gold. Maps, hidden chests and dangerous Werewolves are all part of the adventure that even manages to turn up the old man who originally buried the gold! Buckle up for some more great laughs and lots of campfire fun. (ISBN 1-893302-88-1 $14.95 + S & H

Drifters: The Final Testament, Volume One, by Michael Silverhawk… Within the DRIFTERS trilogy is a powerful secret, a key that unlocks our human potential! Can one man "make a difference" not only in his own life but for everyone else on the planet? Is it possible for a single human to transform chaos into order, darkness into light? (ISBN 1-893302-57-1) - $22.95 + S & H

Ticket to Paradise, by Yvonne Ridley…Judith Tempest, a British reporter, is searching for the Truth. But when it starts to spill out in her brilliant front page reportage of Middle East suicide bombing in retaliation for Israeli tanks mowing down innocent Palestinian women and children, both 'Tempest' and 'Truth' start to spell 'Trouble'— with a capital 'T', joke her friends and colleagues. A non-stop mystery thriller that tears along at a reckless pace of passion, betrayal, adventure and espionage. (ISBN 1-893302-77-6) $17.95 + S & H

Synchronicity Gates: An Anthology Of Stories And Poetry About People Transformed In Extraordinary Reality Beyond Experience, by Stephen Vernarelli… An inventive compilation of short stories that take the reader beyond mere science, fiction, or fantasy. Vernarelli introduces the reader to a new perception of reality; he imagines the best and makes it real. (ISBN 1-893302-38-5) - $17.95 + S & H

The Alley of Wishes, by Laurel Johnson… Despite the ravages of WWI on Paris and on the young American farm boy, Beck Sanow, and despite the abusive relationship that the chanteuse Cerise endures, the two share a bond that is unbreakable by time, war, loss of memory, loss of life and loss of youth. Beck and Cerise are both good people beset by constant tragedy. Yet it is tragedy that brings them together, and it is unconditional love that keeps them together. (ISBN 1-893302-46-6) - $17.95 + S & H

Freedom: Letting Go Of Anxiety And Fear Of The Unknown, by Jim Britt... Jeremy Carter, a fireman from Missouri who is in New York City for the day, decides to take a tour of the Trade Center, only to watch in shock, the attack on its twin towers from a block away. Afterward as he gazes at the pit of rubble and talks with many of the survivors, Jeremy starts to explore the inner depths of his soul, to ask questions he'd never asked before. This dialogue helps him learn who he is and what it takes to overcome the fear, anger, grief and anxiety this kind of tragedy brings. (ISBN 1-893302-74-1) - $18.95 + S & H

The Prince Must Die, by Gower Leconfield... breaks all taboos for mystery thrillers. After the "powers that be" suppressed the manuscripts of three major British writers, Dandelion Books breaks through with a thriller involving a plot to assassinate Prince Charles. *The Prince Must Die* brings to life a Britain of today that is on the edge with race riots, neo-Nazis, hard right backlash and neo-punk nihilists. Riveting entertainment... you won't be able to put it down. (ISBN 1-893302-72-5) -$14.95 + S & H

Come as You Are, by Sarah Daniels... "Tongue-in-cheek" entertainment at its wackiest—and most subtle. If anyone ever doubted that sex makes the world go around, author Sarah Daniels will put your mind, and body to test. Non-stop humor, humanness and wisdom are bundled together to deliver one of life's most important unheeded lessons: each of us has a unique destiny to discover, and until we find and embark on that destiny, life may be one bowl of cherry pits after another. Adult language and scenes. (ISBN 1-893302-15-6) - $14.95 + S & H

Unfinished Business, by Elizabeth Lucas Taylor... Lindsay Mayer knows something is amiss when her husband, Griffin, a college professor, starts spending too much time at his office and out-of-town. Shortly after the ugly truth surfaces, Griffin disappears altogether. Lindsay is shattered. Life without Griffin is life without life... One of the sexiest books you'll ever read! (ISBN 1-893302-68-7) - $14.95 + S & H

The Woman With Qualities, by Sarah Daniels... South Florida isn't exactly the Promised Land that forty-nine-year-old newly widowed Keri Anders had in mind when she transplanted herself here from the northeast... A tough action-packed novel that is far more than a love story. (ISBN 1-893302-11-3) - $14.95 + S & H

Adventure Capital, by John Rushing...South Florida adventure, crime and violence in a fiction story based on a true life experience. A book you will not want to put down until you reach the last page.

(ISBN 1-893302-08-3) $14.95 + S & H

A Mother's Journey: To Release Sorrow And Reap Joy, by Sharon Kay... A poignant account of Norah Ann Mason's life journey as a wife, mother and single parent. This book will have a powerful impact on anyone, female or male, who has experienced parental abuse, family separations, financial struggles and a desperate need to find the magic in life that others talk about that just doesn't seem to be there for them. (ISBN 1-893302-52-0) - $16.95 + S & H

Return To Masada, by Robert G. Makin... In a gripping account of the famous Battle of Masada, Robert G. Makin skillfully recaptures the blood and gore as well as the spiritual essence of this historic struggle for freedom and independence. (ISBN 1-893302-10-5) $18.95 + S & H

Time Out Of Mind, by Solara Vayanian... Atlantis had become a snake pit of intrigue teeming with factious groups vying for power and control. An unforgettable drama that tells of the breakdown of the priesthood, the hidden scientific experiments in genetic engineering which produced "things" — part human and part animal — and other atrocities; the infiltration by the dark lords of Orion; and the implantation of the human body with a device to fuel the Orion wars. (ISBN 1-893302-21-0) $16.95 + S & H

ALL DANDELION BOOKS ARE AVAILABLE THROUGH *WWW.DANDELIONBOOKS.NET*... ALWAYS. NEW:

TOLL-FREE ORDERS 1-800-861-7899 (U.S. & CANADA)

Printed in the United States
64659LVS00002B/55-102

9 781893 302945